Incubi and Succubi
or Demoniality

Incubi and Succubi or Demoniality
A Historical Study of Sexual Contacts with Demons
Author: Sinistrari of Ameno

Original title: *De Dæmonialitate, et Incubis, et Succubis*
Cover image: *The Nightmare or Incubus* (detail), 1781, Henri Fuseli
Lay-out: www.burokd.nl

ISBN 978-94-92355-26-3

VAMzzz Publishing
P.O. Box 3340
1001 AC Amsterdam
The Netherlands
www.vamzzz.com
contactvamzzz@gmail.com

INCUBI and SUCCUBI
or DEMONIALITY
A Historical Study of
Sexual Contacts with Demons

Sinistrari of Ameno
– Revised Edition –

VAMzzz PUBLISHING

(Right: Cover second edition of the French translation by Liseux in 1876)

DE LA
Démonialité

ET DES ANIMAUX
INCUBES ET SUCCUBES

*où l'on prouve qu'il existe sur terre des créatures
raisonnables autres que l'homme, ayant comme lui
un corps et une âme, naissant et mourant comme
lui, rachetées par N.-S. Jésus-Christ et capables
de salut ou de damnation,*

PAR LE R. P.

LOUIS MARIE SINISTRARI D'AMENO

de l'Ordre des Mineurs Réformés de l'étroite Observance
de Saint-François (XVIIe siècle)

*Publié d'après le Manuscrit original découvert
à Londres en 1872 et traduit du Latin par*

ISIDORE LISEUX

SECONDE ÉDITION

PARIS
Isidore LISEUX, 5, Rue Scribe
1876

5

Ludovico Maria Sinistrari
Ameno, Italy, February 26, 1622 – 1701

contents

7

Post Scriptum

Editor's note

THIS VOLUME IS the revised edition of 17th Century work *De Dæ-monialitate, et Incubis, et Succubis* by the French-Italian priest and author Ludovico Maria Sinistrari de Ameno (26 February 1622 – 1701). The Latin text was translated into French & English and published by Isodore Liseux (1835 - 1894). This was Liseux's first 'officiel' publication. He discovered the manuscript himself whilst living in London in 1872. According to the Introduction, Liseux was befriended with a bookseller named "Mr. Allen, a venerable old gentleman, whose place of business was in the Euston road, close to the gate of Regent's park" who had purchased the MS in the auction at Sotheby's in December of 1871 of the library of Baron Seymour Kirkup. The description in the Sotheby catalogue is as follows:

– No 145. Ameno *(R. P. Ludovicus Maria* [Cotta] de) De Dæmonialitate, et Incubis, et Succubis, *Manuscript.* Sœc. XVII-XVIII.

The English translation, published in 1879 as *Demoniality or Incubi and Succubi*, is an extraordinary interesting work the contexts of history, theology, sexology, psychology and occultism, especially demonology. However, 19th Century standards for readability are not the ones we are used to in the 21st Century. This meant that – without notable changes regarding the content – we thoroughly revised the 1879-edition. Mainly by doing "logistics" like separating the original Latin text from the English translation and by upgrading the list of contents, as the work is divided not in chapters but in thematic paragraphs or clusters of paragraphs, more or less presented as small chapters in the original translation. We also put the content list in front of the book (in the original it is found at the end of the work). Finally as VAMzzz Publishing-readers are used to, we gave this book an extra upgrade by adding a Post Sciptum with extra information about the Incubus Succubus phenomenon from several actual sources. In contrast to what some modern scholars believe, this phenomenon cannot be reduced to phantasy or superstition or some maniacal obsession of a Renaissance inquisitor. Today people are still experiencing encounters with what one would describe as a sex demon or sexual astral assault, and not by definition negative or frightening. Many parts of this work are therefore more clarifying and interesting than the modern academic approach of the subject.

Benjamin Adamah,
Editor VAMzzz Publishing – Amsterdam, July 12, 2017

Preface
to the First Edition (Paris, 1875, in-8°)

I WAS IN London in the year 1872, and I hunted after old books: *Car que faire là bas, à moins qu'on ne bouquine?*

They caused me to live in past ages, happy to escape from the present, and to exchange the petty passions of the day for the peaceable intimacy of Aldus, Dolet or Estienne. One of my favourite booksellers was Mr. Allen, a venerable old gentleman, whose place of business was in the Euston road, close to the gate of Regent's park. Not that his shop was particularly rich in dusty old books; quite the reverse: it was small, and yet never filled. Scarcely four or five hundred volumes at a time, carefully dusted, bright, arrayed with symmetry on shelves within reach of one's hand; the upper shelves remained unoccupied. On the right, Theology; on the left, the Greek and Latin Classics in a majority, with some French and Italian books; for such were Mr Allen's specialties; it seemed as if he absolutely ignored Shakespeare and Byron, and as if, in his mind, the literature of his country did not go beyond the sermons of Blair or Macculloch.

What, at first sight, struck one most in those books, was the moderateness of their price, compared with their excellent state of preservation. They had evidently not been bought in a lot, at so much a cubic yard, like the rubbish of an auction, and yet the handsomest, the most ancient, the most venerable from their size, folios or quartos, were not marked higher than 2 or 3 shillings; an octavo was sold l shilling, the duodecimo six pence: each according to its size. Thus ruled Mr Allen, a methodical man, if ever there was one; and he was all the better for it, since, faithfully patronized by clergymen, scholars and collectors, he renewed his stock at a rate which more assuming speculators might have envied.

But how did he get those well bound and well preserved volumes, for which, everywhere else, five or six times more would have been charged? Here also Mr Allen had his method, sure and regular. No one attended more assiduously the auctions which take place every day in London: his stand was marked at the foot of the auctioneer's desk. The rarest, choicest books passed before his eyes, contended for at often fabulous prices by Quaritch, Sotheran, Pickering, Toovey, and other bibliopolists of the British metropolis; Mr. Allen smiled at such extravagance; when once a bid had been made by another, he would not add a penny, had an unknown *Gutenberg* or *Valdarfer's Boccaccio* been at stake. But if occasionally, through inattention or weariness, competition slackened (*habent sua fata libelli*), Mr Allen came forward: *six pence!*, he whispered, and sometimes the article was left him; sometimes even, two consecutive numbers, joined together for want of having separately met with a buyer, were knocked down to him, still for the minimum of six pence which was his maximum.

Many of those slighted ones doubtless deserved their fate; but among them might slip some that were not unworthy of the honours of the catalogue, and which, at any other time, buyers more attentive, or less whimsical might perhaps have covered with gold. This, however, did not at all enter into Mr Allen's calculation: the size was the only rule of his estimate.

Now, one day when, after a considerable auction, he had exhibited in his shop purchases more numerous than usual, I especially noticed some manuscripts in the Latin language, the paper, the writing and the binding of which denoted an Italian origin, and which might well be two hundred years old. The title of one was, I believe: *De Venenis*; of another: *De Viperis*; of a third (the present work): *De Demonialitate, et Incubis, et Succubis*. All three, moreover, by different authors, and independent of each other. Poisons, adders, demons, what a collection of horrors! yet, were it but for civility's sake, I was bound to buy something; after some hesitation, I chose the last one: Demons, true, but Incubi, Succubi: the subject is not vulgar, and still less so the way in which it seemed to me to have been handled. In short, I had the volume for six-pence, a boon price for a quarto: Mr Allen doubtless deemed such a scrawl beneath the rate of type.

That manuscript, on strong paper of the 17th century, bound in Italian parchment, and beautifully preserved, has 86 pages of text. The title and first page are in the author's hand, that of an old man; the remainder is very distinctly written by another, but under his direction, as is testified by autographic side notes and rectifications distributed all through the work. It is therefore the genuine original manuscript, to all appearances unique and inedited.

Our dealer in old books had purchased it a few days before at Sotheby's House, where had taken place (from the 6th to the 16th of

December 1871) the sale of the books of baron Seymour Kirkup, an English collector, deceased in Florence. The manuscript was inscribed as follows on the sale catalogue:

No 145. Ameno (*R. P. Ludovicus Maria* [Cotta] de' De Daemoni-alitate, et Incubis, et Succubis, *Manuscript. Sæc. XVII-XVIII.*

Who is that writer? Has he left printed works? That is a question I leave to bibliographers; for, notwithstanding numerous investigations in special dictionaries, I have been unable to ascertain anything on that score. Brunet (*Manuel du libraire*, art. Cotta d'Ameno) vaguely surmises his existence, but confuses him with his namesake, most likely also his fellow-townsman, Lazaro Agostino Cotta of Ameno, a barrister and literary man of Novara. The author, "says he," whose real Christian names would seem to be Ludovico- Maria, has written many serious works.

The mistake is obvious. One thing is sure: our author was living in the last years of the Iytii century, as appears from his own testimony, and had been a professor of Theology in Pavia.

Be that as it may, his book has seemed to me most interesting in divers respects, and I confidently submit it to that select public for whom the invisible world is not a chimera. I should be much surprised if, after opening it at random, the reader was not tempted to retrace his steps and go on to the end. The philosopher, the confessor, the medical man will find therein, in conjunction with the robust faith of the middle ages, novel and ingenious views; the literary man, the curioso, will appreciate the solidity of reasoning, the clearness of style, the liveliness of recitals (for there are stories, and delicately told). All theologians have devoted more or less pages to the question of material intercourse between man and the demon; thick volumes have been written about witchcraft, and the merits of this work were but slender if it merely developed the ordinary thesis; but such is not its characteristic. The ground-matter, from which it derives a truly original and philosophical stamp, is an entirely novel demonstration of the existence of Incubi and Succubi, as rational animals, both corporeal and spiritual like ourselves, living in our midst, being born and dying like us, and' lastly redeemed, as we are, through the merits of Jesus-Christ, and capable of receiving salvation or damnation. In the Father of Ameno's opinion, those beings endowed with senses and reason, thoroughly distinct from Angels and Demons, pure spirits, are none other but the Fauns, Sylvans and Satyrs of paganism, continued by our Sylphs, Elfs and Goblins; and thus is connected anew the link of belief. On this score alone, not to mention the interest of details, this book has a claim to the attention of earnest readers: I feel convinced that attention will not be found wanting.

I. L.

May 1875.

The foregoing advertisement was composed at the printer's, and ready for the press, when, strolling on the quays (Paris Embankment), I met by chance with a copy of the *Index librovum prohibitorum*. I mechanically opened it, and the first thing that struck my eyes was the following article: De Ameno Ludovicus Maria. Vide Sinistrari. My heart throbbed fast, I must confess. Was I at last on the trace of my author? Was it *Demoniality* that I was about to see nailed to the pillory of

the *Index*? I flew to the last pages of the formidable volume, and read: Sinistrari (Ludovicus Maria) de Ameno, De Delictis et Pœnis Tractatus absolutissimus. Donee corrigatur. Decret. 4 Martii 1709.
Correctus autem juxta editionem Romanam anni 1753 permittitur.

It was indeed he. The real name of the Father of Ameno was *Sinistrari*, and I was in possession of the title of one at least of those "serious works" which Brunet the bibliographer alluded to. The very title, *De Delictis et Pœnis*, was not unconnected with that of my manuscript, and I had reason to presume that Demoniality was one of the offenses inquired into, and decided upon, by Father Sinistrari; in other words, that manuscript, to all appearances inedited, was perhaps published in the extensive work revealed to me; perhaps even was it to that monography of *Demoniality* that the *Tractatus de Delictis et Pœnis* owed its condemnation by the Congregation of the Index. All those points required looking into.

But it is necessary to have attempted investigations of that kind in order to appreciate the difficulties thereof. I consulted the catalogues of ancient books that came in my way; I searched the back-shops of the dealers in old books, the *antiquaries*, as they say in Germany, addressing especially to the two or three firms who in Paris apply themselves to old Theology; I wrote to the principal booksellers in London, Milan, Florence, Rome, Naples: all to no purpose; the very name of Father Sinistrari of Ameno seemed to be unknown. I should perhaps have begun by enquiring at our National Library; I was obliged to resort to it, and there at least I obtained an incipient gratification. I was shown two works by my author: a quarto of

1704, *De incorrigibilium expulsione ab Ordinibus Regularibus*, and the first tome of a set of his complete works: *R. P. Ludovici Mavice Sinistrari de Ameno Opera omnia [Romæ, in domo Caroli Giannini, 1753-1754, 3 vol. in-folio).* Unfortunately that first tome contained but the *Practica Criminalis Minorum illustrata; De Delictis et Pœnis* was the subject matter of the third tome, which, as well as the second, was missing at the Library.

Yet, I had a positive indication, and I pursued my investigations. I might be more fortunate at the Library of St Sulpice Seminary. True, it is not open to the public; but then, the Sulpician Fathers are hospitable: did they not of yore afford a refuge to repentant Des Grieux, and did not Manon Lescaut herself tread the flags of their parlour?! therefore ventured into ihe holy House; it was half past twelve, dinner was nearly over; I asked for the librarian, and after a few minutes, I saw coming to me a short old man, unexceptionably civil, who, leading me through the common parlour, introduced me into another much narrower, a mere cell, looking into a gallery and glazed full breadth, being thus exposed to every eye. An ingenious provision of which Des Grieux's escape had fully shown the urgency. I had no small trouble in explaining the object of my visit to the good Father, who was deaf and near sighted'. He left me to go to the library, and soon returned, but empty handed: there also, in that sanctuary of Catholic Theology, Father Sinistrari of Ameno was entirely unknown. But one more expedient could I try: namely, to go to his brothers in St Francis, the Capuchin Fathers, in their convent of rue de la Santel A cruel extremity, it will be granted, for I had but little chance of meeting there, as here, the lovely shadow of Manon.

At last a letter from Milan put an end to my perplexity. The unfindable book was found; l received at the same time the first edition of *De Delictis et Pœnis {Venetiis, apud Hieronymum Albricium,* 1700), and the edition of *Rome,* 1754. It was a complete treatise, tractatus absolutissimus, upon all imaginable crimes, offenses and sins; but, let us hasten to say, in both those voluminous folios, Demoniality occupies scarcely five pages, without any difference in the text between the two editions. And those five pages are not even a summary of the manuscript work which l now give forth; they only contain the proposition and conclusion (N's l to 27 and 112 to 11 5). As for that wherein lies the originality of the book, to wit the theory of rational animals, Incubi and Succubi, endowed like ourselves with a body and soul, and capable of receiving salvation and damnation, it were vain to look for it. Thus, after so many endeavours, l had settled all the points which l had intended to elucidate: l had discovered the identity of the Father of Ameno(i); from the comparison of the two editions of *De Delictis et Pœnis,* the first condemned, the second allowed by the Congregation of the Index, l had gathered that the printed fragments of *Demoniality* had nothing to do with the condemnation of the *Biographical Notice* at the end of this volume. book, since they had not been submitted to any correction; lastly, l had become convinced that, save a few pages, my manuscript was absolutely inedited. A happy event of a bibliographical Odyssey which l shall be excused for relating at length, for the "jollification" of bibliophiles "and none other".

Isidore Liseux, August 1875.

DEMONIALITY

1.

The first author, who to my knowledge, invented the
word *Demoniality* is John Caramuel, in his *Fundamental Theology*,
and before him I find no one who distinguished that crime from
Bestiality. Indeed, all theological moralists, following in the train
of S. Thomas (2, 2, question 154), include under the specific title
of *Bestiality*, *"every kind of carnal intercourse with anything
whatever of a different species"*: such are the very words used
by S. Thomas. Cajetanus, for instance, in his commentary on
that question, classes intercourse with the Demon under the
description of Bestiality; so does Sylvester, de *Luxuria*, Bonacina,
de Matrimonio, question 4, and others.

2.

However it is clear that in the above passage St. Thomas did not at
all allude to intercourse with the Demon. As shall be demonstrated
further on, that intercourse cannot be included in the very
particular species of *Bestiality*; and, in order to make that sentence

of the holy Doctor tally with truth, it must be admitted that when saying of the unnatural sin, *"that committed through intercourse with a thing of different species, it takes the name of Bestiality"*, St. Thomas, by *a thing of different species*, means a living animal, of another species than man: for he could not here use the word thing in its most general sense, to mean indiscriminately an animate or inanimate being. In fact, if a man should fornicate *cum cadavere humano*, he would have to do with a thing of a species quite different from his own (especially according to the Thomists, who deny the form of human corporeity in a corpse); similarly *si cadaveri bestiali copularetur*: and yet, *talis coitus* would not be bestiality, but pollution. What therefore St. Thomas intended here to specify with -preciseness, is carnal intercourse with a living thing of a species different from man, that is to say, with a beast, and he never in the least thought of intercourse with the Demon.

3.

Therefore, intercourse with the Demon, whether Incubus or Succabus (which is, properly speaking, *Demoniality*) differs in kind from Bestiality, and does not in connection with it form one very particular species, as Cajetanus wrongly gives it; for, whatever may have said to the contrary some Ancients, and later Caramuel in his *Fundamental Theology*, unnatural sins differ from each other most distinctly. Such at least is the general doctrine, and the contrary opinion has been condemned by Alexander VII: first, because each of those sins carries with itself its peculiar and distinct disgrace, repugnant to chastity and to human generation;

secondly, because the commission thereof entails each time the sacrifice of some good by its nature attached to the institution of the venereal act, the normal end of which is human generation; lastly, because they each have a different motive which in itself is sufficient to bring about, in divers ways, the deprivation of the same good, as has been clearly shown by Fillucius, Grespinus and Caramuel.

4.

It follows that *Demoniality* differs in kind from Bestiality, for each has its peculiar and distinct disgrace, repugnant to chastity and human generation. Bestiality is connection with a living beast, endowed with its own peculiar senses and impulses; *Demoniality*, on the contrary, is copulation with a corpse (according at least to the general doctrine which shall be considered hereafter), a senseless and motionless corpse which is but accidentally moved through the power of the Demon. Now, if fornication with the corpse of a man, a woman, or a beast differs in kind from Sodomy and Bestiality, there is the same difference with regard to *Demoniality*, which, according to general opinion, is the intercourse of man with a corpse accidentally set in motion.

5.

Another proof: in sins against nature, the unnatural semination (which cannot be regularly followed by generation) is a genus; but the object of such semination is the difference which marks the species under the genus. Thus, whether semination takes place on the ground, or on an inanimate body, it is pollution; *if cum homine in vase præpostero*, it is Sodomy; with a beast, bestiality: crimes which unquestionably all differ from each other in species, just as the ground, the corpse, the man and the beast, passive objects *talis seminationis*, differ in species from each other. But the difference between the Demon and the beast is not only specific, it is more than specific: the nature of the one is corporeal, of the other incorporeal, which makes a generic difference. Whence it follows that *seminationes* practised on different objects differ in species from each other: and that is substantiated.

6.

It is also a trite doctrine with Moralists, established by the Council of Trent, session 14, and admitted by Theologians, that in confession it suffices to state the circumstances which alter the species of sins. If therefore *Demoniality* and Bestiality belonged to the same very particular species, it would be enough that, each time he has fornicated with the Demon, the penitent should say to his confessor: I have been guilty of the sin of Bestiality. But that is not so: therefore those two sins do not both belong to the same very particular species.

7.

It may be urged that if the circumstances of a sensual intercourse with the Demon should be revealed to the Confessor, it is on account of its offense against Religion, an offense which comes either from the worship rendered to the Demon, or from the homage or prayers offered up to him, or from the compact of fellowship entered into with him (*St. Thomas*, quest. 90). But, as will be seen hereafter, there are Incubi and Succubi to whom none of the foregoing applies, and yet *copula sequitur*. There is consequently, in that special case, no element of irreligion, no other character *quam puri et simplicis coitus*; and, if of the same species as Bestiality, it would be adequately stated by saying: *I have been guilty of the sin of Bestiality*; which is not so.

8.

Besides, it is acknowledged by all theological moralists *that copula cum* Dæmone is much more grievous than the same act committed with any beast soever. Now, in the same very particular species of sins, one sin is not more grievous than another; all are equally so: it comes to the same whether connection is had with a bitch, an ass, or a mare; whence it follows that if *Demoniality* is more grievous than Bestiality, those two acts are not of the same species. And let it not be argued, with Cajetahus, that *Demoniality* is more grievous on account of the offense to religion from the worship rendered to the Demon or the compact of fellowship entered into with him: as has been shown above, that is not always met with in the connection of man with Incubi and Succubi; moreover, if in the genus of unnatural sin *Demoniality* is more grievous than Bestiality, the offense to Religion is quite foreign to that aggravation, since it is foreign to that genus itself.

9.

Now, having laid down the specific difference between *Demoniality* and Bestiality, so that the gravity thereof may be duly appreciated in view of the penalty to be inflicted (and that is our most essential object), We must inquire in how many different ways the sin of *Demoniality* may be committed. There is no lack of people who, infatuated with their small baggage of knowledge, venture to deny what has been written by the gravest authors and is testified by every day experience: namely, that the Demon, whether Incubus or Succubus, unites carnally not only with men and women, but also with beasts. They allege that it all comes from the human imagination troubled by the craft of the Demon, and that there is nothing in it but phantasmagoria and diabolical spells. The like happens, they say, to Witches or Sagas, who, under the influence of an illusion brought on by the Demon, fancy that they attend the nightly sports, dances, revels and vigils, and have carnal intercourse with the Demon, though in reality they are not bodily transferred to those places nor taking part in those deeds, as has been defined verbatim by a Capitule and two Councils.

10.

Of course, it is not contested that sometimes young women, deceived by the Demon, fancy taking part, in their flesh and blood, in the nightly vigils of Witches, without its being anything but an imaginary vision. Thus, in a dream, one sometimes fancies *cum foemina aliqua concumbere, et semen vere excernitur, non tamen concubitus ille realis est*, but merely fantastic, and often brought about by a diabolical illusion: and here the above mentioned Capitule and Councils are perfectly right. But this is not always the case; on the contrary, it more often happens that Witches are bodily present at nightly vigils and have with the Demon a genuine carnal and corporeal connection, and that likewise Wizards copulate with the Succuba or female Demon. Such is the opinion of Theologians as well as of jurists, whose names will be found at length in the *Compendium Maleficarum*, or *Chronicle of Witches*, by Brother Francis Marie Guaccius. This doctrine is therein confirmed by eighteen instances adduced from the recitals of learned and truthful men whose testimony is beyond suspicion, and which prove that Wizards and Witches are indeed bodily present at vigils and most shamefully copulate with Demons, Incubi or Succubi. And, after all, to settle the question, we have the authority of St. Augustine, who, speaking of carnal intercourse between men and the Demon, expresses himself as follows, book 15th, chapt, 23rd of the *City of God*: *"It is widely credited, and such belief is confirmed by the direct or indirect testimony of thoroughly trustworthy people, that Sylvans and Fauns, commonly called Incubi, have frequently molested women, sought and obtained from them coition. There are even Demons, whom the Gauls call Duses or Elfs, who very regularly indulge in those unclean practices: the fact is testified by so many and such weighty authorities, that it were impudent to doubt it."* Such are the very words of St. Augustine.

11.

Now, several authors profess, and it is confirmed by numerous experiments, that the Demon has two ways of copulating carnally with men or women: the one which it uses with Witches or Wizards, the other with men or women entirely foreign to witchcraft.

12.

In the first case, the Demon does not copulate with Witches or Wizards until after a solemn profession, in virtue of which such wretched human beings yield themselves up to him. According to several authors who have related the judicial admissions of Witches when on the rack, and whose recitals have been collected by Francis-Marie Guaccius, *Compend. Malef.*, book I, chapt. 7, that profession consists of eleven ceremonials:

13.

Firstly, the Novices have to conclude with the Demon, or some other Wizard or Magician acting in the Demon's place, an express compact by which, in the presence of witnesses, they enlist in the Demon's service, he giving them in exchange his pledge for honours, riches and carnal pleasures.

14.

Secondly, they abjure the catholic faith, withdraw from the obedience to God, renounce Christ and the protection of the most blessed Virgin Mary, and all the Sacraments of the Church.

15.

Thirdly, they cast away the Crown, or Rosary of the most blessed Virgin Mary, the girdle of S. Francis, or the strap of S. Austin, or the scapular of the Carmelites, should they belong to one of those Orders, the Cross, the Medals, the *Agnus Dei*, whatever other holy or consecrated object may have been about their person, and trample them all under foot.

16.

Fourthly, in the hands of the Devil they vow obedience and subjection; they pay him homage and vassalage, laying their fingers on some very black book. They bind themselves never to return to the faith of Christ, to observe none of the divine precepts, to do no good work, but to obey the Demon alone and, to attend diligently the nightly conventicles.

17.

Fifthly, they promise to strive with all their power, and to give their utmost zeal and care for the enlistment of other males and females in the service of the Demon.

18.

Sixthly, the Devil administers to them a kind of sacrilegious baptism, and after abjuring their Godfathers and Godmothers of the Baptism of Christ and Confirmation, they have assigned to them a new Godfather and a new Godmother, who are to instruct them in the arts of witchcraft; they drop their former name and exchange it for another, more frequently a scurrilous nickname.

19.

Seventhly, they cut off a part of their own garments, and tender it as a token of homage to the Devil, who takes it away and keeps it.

20.

Eighthly, the Devil draws on the ground a circle wherein stand the Novices, Witches and Wizards, and there they confirm by oath all their aforesaid promises.

21.

Ninthly, they request the Devil to strike them out of the book of Christ, and to inscribe them in his own. Then comes forth that very black book on which, as has been said before, they laid hands when doing homage, and they are inscribed therein with the Devil's claw.

22.

Tenthly, they promise the Devil sacrifices and offerings at stated times: once a fortnight or at least each month, the murder of some child, or an homicidal act of sorcery, and other weekly misdeeds to the prejudice of mankind, such as hailstorms, tempests, fires, cattle plagues, etc.

23.

Eleventhly, the Demon imprints on them some mark, especially on those whose constancy he suspects. That mark, moreover, is not always of the same shape or figure: sometimes it is the image of a hare, sometimes a toad's leg, sometimes a spider, a puppy, a dormouse. It is imprinted on the most hidden parts of the body: with men, under the eye-lids, or the armpits, or the lips, on the shoulder, the fundament, or somewhere else; with women, it is usually on the breasts or the privy parts. Now, the stamp which imprints those marks is none other but the Devil's claw. This having been all performed in accordance with the instructions of the Teachers who have initiated the Novices, these promise lastly never to worship the Eucharist; to insult all Saints and especially the most blessed Virgin Mary; to trample under foot and vilify the holy images, the Cross and the relics of Saints; never to use the sacraments or sacramental ceremonials; never to make a full confession to the priest, but to keep always hidden from him their intercourse with the Demon. The Demon, in exchange, engages to give them always prompt assistance; to fulfill their desires in this world and to make them happy after their death. The solemn profession being thus performed, each has assigned to himself a Devil, called *Magistellus* or Assistant Master, with whom he retires in private for carnal satisfaction; the said Devil being, of course, in the shape of a woman if the initiated person is a man, in the shape of a man, sometimes of a satyr, sometimes of a buck-goat, if it is a woman who has been received a witch.

24.

If the authors be asked how it comes to pass that the Demon, who has no body, yet has carnal intercourse with man or woman, they unanimously answer that the Demon assumes the corpse of another human being, male or female as the case may be, or that, from the mixture of other materials, he shapes for himself a body endowed with motion, and by means of which he is united with the human being; and they add that when women are desirous of becoming pregnant by the Demon (which only occurs by the consent and express wish of the said women), the Demon is transformed into a Succuba, *et juncta homini semen ab eo recipit*; or else he procures pollution from a man during his sleep, *et semen prolectum in suo nativo calore, et cum vitali spiritu conservat, et incubando foemince infert in ipsius matricem*, whence follows impregnation. Such is the teaching of Guaccius, book 1, chapt. 12, who supports it on a number of quotations and instances taken from various Doctors.

25.

At other times also the Demon, whether Incubus or Succubus, copulates with men or women from whom he receives none of the sacrifices, homage or offerings which he is wont to exact from Wizards or Witches, as aforesaid. He is then but a passionate lover, having only one desire: the carnal possession of the loved ones. Of this there are numerous instances to be found in the authors, amongst which the case of Menippus Lycius, who, after frequent coition with a woman, was by her entreated to marry her; but a certain philosopher, who partook of the wedding entertainment, having guessed what that woman was, told Menippus that he had to deal with a *Compusa*, that is a Succuba Demon; whereupon the bride vanished bewailing: such is the narrative given by Coelius Rhodiginus, Antiq., book 29, chapt. 5. Hector Boethius (*Hist. Scot.*) also relates the case of a young Scot, who, during many months, with closed doors and windows, was visited in his bedroom by a Succuba Demon of the most bewitching beauty; caresses, kisses, embraces, entreaties, she resorted to every blandishment *ut secum coiret*: but she could not prevail on the chaste young man.

26.

We read likewise of numerous women incited to coition by the Incubus Demon, and who, though reluctant at first of yielding to him, are soon moved by his entreaties, tears and endearments; he is a desperate lover and must not be denied. And although this comes sometimes of the craft of some Wizard who avails himself of the agency of the Demon, yet the Demon not infrequently acts on his own account; and it happens not merely with women, but also with mares; if they readily comply with his desire, he pets them, and plaits their mane in elaborate and inextricable tresses; but if they resist, he ill-treats and strikes them, smites them with the glanders, and finally puts them to death, as is shown by daily experience.

27.

A most marvelous and well high incomprehensible fact: the Incubi whom the Italians call *Folletti*, the Spaniards *Duendes*, the French *Follets*, do not obey the Exorcists, have no dread of exorcisms, no reverence for holy things, at the approach of which they are

not in the least overawed; very different in that respect from the
Demons who vex those whom they possess; for, however obstinate
those evil Spirits may be, however restive to the injunctions of the
Exorcist who bids them leave the body they possess, yet, at the
mere utterance of the most holy name of Jesus or Mary, or of some
verses of Holy Writ, at the mere imposition of relics, especially
of a piece of the wood of the Holy Cross, or the sight of the holy
images, they roar at the mouth of the possessed person, they
gnash, shake, quiver, and display fright and awe. But the Folletti
show none of those signs, and leave off their vexations but after a
long space of time. Of this I was an eye-witness, and shall relate a
story which verily passes human belief: but I take God to witness
that I tell the precise truth, corroborated by the testimony of
numerous persons.

28.

About twenty five years ago, when I was a lecturer on Sacred
Theology in the convent of the Holy Cross, in Pavia, there was
living in that city a married woman of unimpeachable morality, and
who was most highly spoken of by all such as knew her, especially
by the Friars; her name was Hieronyma, and she lived in the parish
of S. Michael. One day, this woman had kneaded bread at home and
given it out to bake. The oven-man brought her back her loaves
when baked, and with them a large cake of a peculiar shape, and
made of butter and Venetian paste, as is usual in that city. She
declined to take it in, saying she had not made any thing of the
kind. — "But", said the oven-man, "I had no other bread, but yours

to bake to-day, therefore this cake also must have come from your house; your memory is at fault". The good lady allowed herself to be persuaded, and partook of the cake with her husband, her little girl three years old, and the house servant. The next night, whilst in bed with her husband, and both asleep, she suddenly woke up at the sound of a very slender voice, something like a shrill hissing, whispering in her ears, yet with great distinctness, and inquiring whether a the "cake had been to her taste?" The good lady, frightened, set about guarding herself with a sign of the cross and repeatedly calling the names of Jesus and Mary. "Be not afraid, said the voice, I mean you no harm; quite the reverse: I am prepared to do anything to please you; I am captivated by your beauty, and desire nothing more than to enjoy your embraces". And she felt somebody kissing her cheeks, so lightly, so softly, that she might have fancied being grazed by the finest down. She resisted without giving any answer, merely repeating over and over again the names of Jesus and Mary, and crossing herself; the tempter kept on thus for nearly half an hour, when he withdrew. The next morning the dame called on her Confessor, a discreet and learned man, who confirmed her in her faith, exhorted her to maintain her energetic resistance and to provide herself with some holy relics. On the ensuing nights, like temptation with the same language and kisses, like constancy also on the part of the woman. Weary however of such painful and persistent molestation, taking the advice of her Confessor and other grave men, she had herself exorcised by experienced Exorcists, in order to ascertain whether perchance she was not possessed. Having found in her no trace of the evil

Spirit, they blessed the house, the bed-room, the bed, and enjoined on the Incubus to discontinue his molestations. All to no purpose: he kept on worse than ever, pretending to be love-sick, weeping and moaning in order to melt the heart of the lady, who however, by the grace of God, remained unconquered. The Incubus then went another way to work: he appeared in the shape of a lad or little man of great beauty, with golden locks, a flaxen beard that shone like gold, sea-green eyes calling to mind the flax-flower, and arrayed in a fancy Spanish dress. Besides he appeared to her even when in company, whimpering, after the fashion of lovers, kissing his hand to her, and endeavouring by every means to obtain her embraces. She alone saw and heard him: for everybody else, he was not to be seen. The good lady kept persevering in her admirable constancy till, at last, after some months of courting, the Incubus, incensed at her disdain, had recourse to a new kind of persecution. First, he took away from her a silver cross filled with holy relics, and a holy wax or papal lamb of the blessed Pontiff Pius V, which she always carried on her person; then, leaving the locks untouched, he purloined her rings and other gold and silver jewelry from the casket wherein they were put away. Next, he began to strike her cruelly, and after each beating bruises and marks were to be seen on her face, her arms or other parts of her body, which lasted a day or two, then suddenly disappeared, the reverse of natural bruises which decrease slowly and by degrees. Sometimes, while she was nursing her little girl, he would snatch the child away from on her breast and lay it upon the roof, on the edge of the gutter, or hide it, but without ever harming it. Sometimes he would upset all the furniture, or smash to pieces saucepans, plates and other earthenware which, in the twinkling of an eye, he restored tho their former state. One night that she was lying with her husband, the Incubus, appearing in his customary shape, vehemently urged his demand which she resisted as usual. The Incubus withdrew in a rage, and shortly came back with a large load of those flag stones which the Genoese, and the inhabitants of Liguriain general, use for roofing their houses. With those stones he built around the bed a wall so high that it reached the tester, and that the couple could not leave their bed without using a ladder. This wall however was built up without lime; when pulled down, the flags were laid by in a corner where, during two days, they were seen by many who came to look at them; they then disappeared. On S. Stephen's day, the husband had asked some military friends to dinner, and, to do honour to his guests, had provided a substantial repast. Whilst they were, as customary, washing their hands before taking their seats, suddenly vanished the table dressed in the dining-room; all the dishes, saucepans, kettles, plates and crockery in the kitchen vanished likewise, as well as the jugs, bottles and glasses. You may imagine the surprise, the stupor of the guests, eight in number; amongst them was a Spanish Captain of infantry, who, addressing the company, said to them: "Do not be frightened, it is but a trick: the table is certainly still where it stood, and I shall soon find it by feeling for it". Having thus spoken, he paced round the room with outstretched arms, endeavouring to lay hold of the table; but when, after many circuitous perambulations, it was apparent that he laboured in vain and grasped at nought but thin air, he was laughed at by his friends; and it being already high time for having dinner, each guest took up his cloak and set about to return home. They had already reached the street-door with the husband, who, out of politeness, was attending them, when they heard a great noise in the dining-room: they stood to ascertain the cause thereof, and presently the servant came up to announce that the kitchen was stocked with new vessels filled with food, and that the table was standing again in its former place. Having gone back to the dining-room, they were stupefied to see the table was laid, with cloths, napkins, salt-cellars, and trays that did not belong to the house, and with food which had not been cooked there. On a large sideboard all were arrayed in perfect order crystal, silver and gold chalices, with all kind of amphoras, decanters and cups filled with foreign wines, from the Isle of Crete, Campania, the Canaries, the Rhine, etc. In the kitchen there was also an abundant variety of meats in saucepans and dishes that had never been seen there before. At first, some of the guests hesitated whether they should taste of that food; however, encouraged by others, they sat down, and soon partook of the meal, which was found exquisite. Immediately afterwards, as they were sitting before a seasonable fire, everything vanished at once, the dishes and the leavings, and in their stead reappeared the cloth of the house and the victual which had been previously cooked; but, for a wonder, all the guests were satisfied, so that no one thought of supper after such a magnificent dinner. A clear proof that the substituted viands were real and nowise fictitious. This kind of persecution had been going on some months, when the lady betook herself to the blessed Bernardine of Feltri, whose body is worshipped in the church of St James, a short distance from the walls of the city. She made a vow to him that she would wear, during a whole twelve-month, a grey frock, tied round her waist with a piece of cord, and such as is worn by the Minor Brethren, the order to which had belonged the blessed Bernardine; this she vowed, in the hope of being, through his intercession, at last rid of the persecution of the Incubus. And accordingly, on the 28th of September, the vigil of the Dedication of the Archangel S. Michael, and the festival of the blessed Bernardine, she assumed the votive robe. The next morning, which was S. Michael's festival, the afflicted woman proceeded to the church of St Michael, her own parish, already mentioned; it was about ten o'clock, a time when a crowd of people were going to mass. She had no sooner set foot on the threshold of the church, than her clothes and ornaments fell off to the ground, and disappeared in a gust of wind, leaving her stark naked. There happened fortunately to be among the crowd two cavaliers of mature age, who, seeing what had taken place, hastened to divest themselves of their cloaks with which they concealed, as well as they could, the woman's nudity, and having put her into a vehicle, accompanied her home. The clothes and trinkets taken by the Incubus were not restored by him before six months had elapsed. I might relate many other most surprising tricks which that Incubus played on her, were it not wearisome. Suffice it to say that, for a number of years he persevered in his temptation of her, but that finding at last that he was losing his pains, he. desisted from his vexatious importunities.

29.

In the above case, as well as in others that may be heard or read of occasionally, the Incubus attempts no act against Religion; he merely assails chastity. In consequence, consent is not a sin through ungodliness, but through incontinence.

30.

Now, it is undoubted by Theologians and philosophers that carnal intercourse between mankind and the Demon sometimes gives birth to human beings; that is how is to be born the Antichrist, according to some Doctors, such as Bellarmin, Suarez, Maluenda, etc. They further observe that, from a natural cause, the children thus begotten by Incubi are tall, very hardy and bold, very proud and wicked. Thus writes Maluenda; as for the cause, he gives it from Vallesius, Archphysician in Reggio: "What Incubi introduce in *uteros, is not qualecumque neque quantum, cumque semen,* but abundant, very thick, very warm, rich in spirits and free from serosity. This moreover is an easy thing for them, since they have but to choose ardent, robust men, *et abundantes multo semine, quibus succumbant,* and then women of a like constitution, *quibus incumbant,* taking care that both shall enjoy *voluptatem solito majorem, tanto enim abundanthis emittitur semen, quanta cum majori voluptate excernitur."* Those are the words of Vallesius, confirmed by Maluenda who shows, from the testimony of various Authors, mostly classical, that such associations gave birth to: Romulus and Remus, according to *Livy* and Plutarch;

Servius-Tullius, the sixth king of Rome, according to *Dyonisius of Halicarnassus* and *Pliny the Elder*; Plato the Philosopher, according to *Diogenes Laertius* and *Saint Hieronymus*; Alexander the Great, according to *Plutarch* and *Quintus-Curtius*; Seleucus, king of Syria, according to *Justinus* and *Appianus*; Scipio Africanus the Elder, according to *Livy*; the emperor Caesar Augustus, according to *Suetonius*; Aristomenes the Messenian, an illustrious Greek commander, according to *Strabo* and *Pausanias*; as also Merlin or Melchin the Englishman, born from an Incubus and a nun, the daughter of Charlemagne; and, lastly, as shown by the writings of Cochlæus quoted by *Maluenda*, that damned Heresiarch ycleped Martin Luther.

31.

However, with due deference to so many and such learned Doctors, I hardly see how their opinion can bear examination. For, as Pererius truly observes in his *Commentary on the Genesis*, chapt. 6, the whole strength and efficiency of the human sperm reside in the spirits which evaporate and vanish as soon as issued from the genital vessels wherein they were warmly stored: ail medical men agree on that point. It is consequently not possible that the Demon should preserve in a fit state for generation the sperm he has received; for it were necessary that whatever vessel he endeavoured to keep it in should be equally warm with the human genital organs, the warmth of which is nowhere to be met with but in those organs themselves. Now, in a vessel where that warmth is not intrinsical but extraneous, the spirits get altered, and no generation can take place. There is this other objection, that generation is a vital act by which man, begetting from his own substance, carries the sperm through natural organs to the spot which is appropriate to generation. On the contrary, in this particular case, the introduction of sperm cannot be a vital act of the man who begets, since it is not carried into the womb by his agency; and, for the same cause, it cannot be said that the man, whose sperm it was, has begotten the fetus which proceeds from it. Nor can the Incubus be deemed its father, since the sperm does not issue from his own substance. Consequentially, a child would be born without a father, which is absurd. Third objection: when the father begets in the course of nature, there is a concurrence of two casualties: the one, material, for he provides the sperm which is the matter of generation; the other, efficient, for he is the principal agent of generation, as Philosophers agree in declaring. But, in this case, the man who only provided the sperm would contribute but a mere material, without any action tending to generation; he could therefore not be regarded as the father of the child begotten under those circumstances; and this is opposed to the notion that the child begotten by an Incubus is not his son, but the son of the man whose sperm the Incubus has taken.

32.

Besides, there is not a shadow of probability in what was written by Vallesius and quoted from him by us (Vide supra, No 3o); and I wonder that anything so extravagant should have fallen from the pen of such a learned man. Medical men are well aware that the size of the fetus depends, not indeed on the quantity of matter, but on the quantity of virtue, that is to say of spirits held by the sperm; there lies the whole secret of generation, as is well observed by Michael Ettmuller, *Institut. Medic. Physiolog.*: "Generation", says he, "entirely depends upon the genital spirit contained within an envelope of thicker matter; that spermatic matter does not remain in the uterus, and has no share in the formation of the fetus; it is but the genital spirit of the male, combined with the genital spirit of the female, that permeates the pores, or, less frequently, the tubes of the uterus, which it fecundates by that means." Of what moment can therefore the quantity of sperm be for the size of the fetus? Besides, it is not always a fact that men thus begotten by Incubi are remarkable for the huge proportions of their body: Alexander the Great, for instance, who is said to have been thus born, as we have mentioned, was very short; as the poet said of him:

Magnus Alexander corpore parvus erat.

Besides, although it is generally a fact that those who are thus begotten excel other men, yet such superiority is not always shown by their vices, but sometimes by their virtues and even their morals; Scipio Africanus, for instance, Caesar Augustus and Plato the Philosopher, as is recorded of each of them respectively by Livy, Suetonius and Diogenes Laertius, had excellent morals. Whence may be inferred that, if other individuals begotten in the same way have been downright villains, it was not owing to their being born of an Incubus, but to their having, of their own free will, chosen to be such. We also read in the Testament, Genesis, chap. 6, verse 4, that giants were born when the sons of God came in unto the daughters of men: that is the very letter of the sacred text. Now, those giants were men of *great stature*, says *Baruch*, chap. 3, verse 26, and far superior to other men. Not only were they distinguished by their huge size, but also by their physical power, their plundering habits and their tyranny. Through their criminal excesses the Giants were the primary and principal cause of the Flood, according to Cornelius a Lapide, in his *Commentary on Genesis*. Some contend that by Sons of God are meant the sons of Seth, and by Daughters of men the daughters of Cain, because the former practiced piety, religion and every other virtue, whilst the descendants of Cain were quite the reverse; but, with all due deference to Chrysostom, Cyrillus, Hilarius and others who are of that opinion, it must be conceded that it clashes with the obvious meaning of the text. Scripture says, in fact, that of the conjunction of the above mentioned were born men of huge bodily size: consequently, those giants were not previously in existence, and if their birth was the result of that conjunction, it cannot be ascribed to the intercourse of the sons of Seth with the daughters of Cain, who being themselves of ordinary stature, could but procreate children of ordinary stature. Therefore, if the intercourse in question gave birth to beings of huge stature, the reason is that it was not the common connection between man and woman, but the performance of Incubi Demons who, from their nature, may very well be styled sons of God. Such is the opinion of the Platonist Philosophers and of Francis Georges the Venetian; nor is it discrepant from that of Josephus the Historian, Philo the Jew, St. Justinus the Martyr, Clement of Alexandria, and Tertullian, who look upon Incubi as corporeal Angels who have allowed themselves to fall into the sin of lewdness with women. Indeed, as shall be shown hereafter, though seemingly distinct, those two opinions are but one and the same.

33.

If therefore these Incubi, in conformity with general belief, have begotten Giants by means of sperm taken from man, it is impossible, as aforesaid, that of that sperm should have been born any but men of approximately the same size as he from whom it came; for it would be in vain for the Demon, when acting the part of a Succubus, to draw from man an unwonted quantity of prolific liquor in order to procreate there from children of higher stature; quantity has nothing to do here, since all depends, as we have said, upon the vitality of that liquor, not its quantity. We are therefore bound to infer that Giants are born of another sperm than man's, and that, consequently, the Incubus Demon, for the purpose of generation, uses a sperm which is not man's. But then, what is to be said?

34.

Subject to correction by our Holy Mother Church, and as a mere expression of opinion, I say that the Incubus Demon, when having intercourse with women, begets the human fetus from his own sperm.

35.

To many that proposition will seem heterodox and hardly sensible; but I beg of my reader not to condemn it precipitately; for if, as Celsus says, it is improper to deliver judgment without having thoroughly inquired into the law, no less unfair is the rejection of an opinion, before the arguments upon which it rests have been weighed and confuted. I have therefore to prove the above conclusion, and must necessarily premise with some statements.

36.

Firstly, I premise, as an article of belief, that there are purely spiritual creatures, not in any way partaking of corporeal matter, as was ruled by the Council of Lateran, under the pontificate of Innocent III. Such are the blessed Angels, and the Demons condemned to ever-lasting fire. Some Doctors, it is true, have professed, subsequently even to this Council, that the spirituality of Angels and Demons is not an article of belief; others even have asserted that they are corporeal, whence Bonaventure Baron has drawn the conclusion that it is neither heretical nor erroneous to ascribe to Angels and Demons a twofold substance, corporeal and spiritual. Yet, the Council having formally declared it to be an article of belief that *God is the maker of all things visible and invisible, spiritual and corporeal, who has raised from nothing every creature spiritual or corporeal. Angelic or terrestrial*, I contend it is an article of belief that there are certain merely spiritual creatures, and that such are Angels; not all of them, but a certain number.

37.

It may seem strange, yet it must be admitted not to be unlikely. If, in fact. Theologians concur in establishing amongst Angels a specific, and therefore essential, diversity so considerable that, according to St. Thomas, there are not two Angels of the same species, but that each of them is a species by himself, why should not certain Angels be most pure spirits, of a consequently very superior nature, and others corporeal, therefore of a less perfect nature, differing thus from each other in their corporeal or incorporeal substance? This doctrine has the advantage of solving the otherwise insoluble contradiction between two (Ecumenical Councils, namely the Seventh General Synod and the abovementioned Council of Lateran. For, during the fifth sitting of that Synod, the second of Nicea, a book was introduced written by John of Thessalonica against a pagan Philosopher, wherein occur the following propositions: *"Respecting Angels, Archangels and their Powers, to which I adjoin our own Souls, the Catholic Church is really of opinion that they are intelligences, hut not entirely bodyless and senseless, as you Gentiles aver; she on the contrary ascribes to them a subtile body, aerial or igneous, according to what is written: He makes the spirits His Angels, and the burning fire His Minister"*. And further on: *"Although not corporeal in the same way as ourselves, made of the four elements, yet it is impossible to say that Angels, Demons and Souls are incorporeal; for they have been seen many a time, invested with their own body, by those whose eyes the Lord had opened"*. And after that book had been read through before all the Fathers in Council assembled, Tharasius, the Patriarch of Constantinople, submitted it to the approval of the Council, with these words: *"The Father showeth that Angels should be pictured, since their form can be defined, and they have been seen in the shape of men"*. Without a dissentient, the Synod answered: "Yes, my Lord".

38.

That this approbation by a Council of the doctrine set forth at length in the book of John establishes an article of belief with regard to the corporeity of Angels, there is not a shadow of doubt: so Theologians toil and moil in order to remove the contradiction apparent between that decision and the definition, above quoted, by the Council of Lateran. One of them, Suarez, says that if the Fathers did not disprove such an assertion of the corporeity of Angels, it is because that was not the question. Another contends that the Synod did approve the conclusion, namely that Angels might be pictured, but not the motive given, *their corporeity*. A third, Molina, observes that the definitions issued in Council by the Synod were thus issued only at the *seventh sitting*, whence he argues that those of the previous sittings are not definitions of belief. Others, lastly, write that neither the Council of Nicea nor that of Lateran intended defining a question of belief, the Council of Nicea having spoken according to the opinion of the Platonists, which describes Angels as corporeal beings and was then prevailing, whilst that of Lateran went with Aristoteles, who, in his 12th book of *Metaphysics*, lays down the existence of incorporeal intelligences, a doctrine which has since carried the day with most

Doctors over the Platonists.

39.

But anyone can discern the invalidity of those answers, and
Bonaventure Baro (Scot. Defens., tome 9) proves to evidence
that they do not bear. In consequence, in order to agree the two
Councils, we must say that the Council of Nicea meant one species
of Angels, and that of Lateran another: the former, corporeal,
the latter on the contrary absolutely incorporeal; and thus are
reconciled two otherwise irreconcilable Councils.

40.

Secondly, I premise that the word Angel applies, not indeed to the
kind, but to the office: the Holy Fathers are agreed thereupon (St.
Ambrose, on the *Epistle to the Hebrews*; St. Augustine, *City of
God*; St. Gregory, *Homily 34 on Scripture*; St. Isidorus, *Supreme
Goodness*). An Angel, very truly says St. Ambrose, is thus styled,
not because he is a spirit, but on account of his office: Ἀγγελος in
Greek, *Nuntius* in Latin, that is to say *Messenger*; it follows that
whoever is entrusted by God with a mission, be he spirit or man,
may be called an Angel, and is thus called in the Holy Scriptures,
where the following words are applied to Priests, Preachers and
Doctors, who, as Messengers of God, explain to men the divine will
(Malachi, chapt. 2, V. 7). "The priest's lips should keep knowledge,
and they should seek the law at his mouth, for he is the Angel of
the Lord of Hosts." The same prophet, chapt. 3, V. I, bestows the
name of Angel on St. John the Baptist, when saying: "*Behold, I will*

send my Angel and he shall prepare the way before me." That this prophecy literally applies to St. John the Baptist is testified by our Lord Jesus Christ, in the Gospel, according to St. Matthew, chapt. 11, V. 10. Still more: God himself is called an Angel, because he has 'been sent by His Father to herald the law of mercy. To witness, the prophecy of Isaiah, chapt. 9, v. 6, according to Septuagint: "*He shall be called an Angel of Wonderful Counsel.*" And more plainly still in Malachi, chapt. 3, v. i: "*The Lord whom ye seek shall suddenly come to his temple, even the Angel of the covenant whom ye delight in*", a prophecy which literally applies to our Lord Jesus-Christ. There is consequently nothing absurd in the contention that some Angels are corporeal, since men, who assuredly have a body, are called Angels.

41.

Thirdly, I premise that neither the existence nor the nature of the natural things in this world has been sufficiently investigated to allow of denying a fact, merely because it has never been previously spoken of or written about. In the course of time have not new lands been discovered which the Ancients knew not of? New animals, herbs, plants, fruits and seeds, never seen elsewhere? And if that mysterious Austral land came at last to be explored, as has been to this day vainly tried by so many travelers, what unforeseen disclosures would be the result! Through the invention of the microscope and other instruments used by modern experimental Philosophy, combined with the more exact methods of investigation of Anatomists, have there not been, and are there not, every day, brought to light the existence, qualities and characteristics of a number of natural things unknown to ancient Philosophers, such as fulminating gold, phosphorus, and a hundred other chemical compounds, the circulation of the blood, the lacteal vessels, the lymphducts and other recent anatomical discoveries? To deride a doctrine because it does not happen to be mentioned in any ancient author would therefore be absurd, especially bearing in mind this axiom of Logic: *locus ab auctoritate negativa non tenet.*

42.

Fourthly, I premise that Holy Scripture and ecclesiastical tradition do not teach us anything beyond what is requisite for the salvation of the soul, namely Faith, Hope and Charity. Consequently, from a thing not being stated either by Scripture or tradition it must not be inferred that that thing is not in existence. For instance, Faith teaches us that God, by His Word, made things visible, and invisible, and also that, through the merits of our Lord Jesus Christ, grace and glory are conferred on every rational creature. Now, that there be another World than the one we live in, and that it be peopled by men not born of Adam but made by God, in some other way, as is implied by those who believe the lunar globe to be inhabited; or further, that in the very World we dwell in, there be other rational creatures besides man and the Angelic Spirits, creatures generally invisible to us and whose being is disclosed but accidentally, through the instrumentality of their own power; all that has nothing to do with Faith, and the knowledge or ignorance thereof is no more necessary to the salvation of man than knowing the number or nature of all physical things.

43.

Fifthly, I premise that neither Philosophy nor Theology is repugnant to the possible existence of rational creatures having spirit and body and distinct from man. Such repugnance could be supported only on God, and that is inadmissible, since he is all-mighty, or on the thing to be made, and that likewise cannot be supported; for, as there are purely spiritual creatures, such as Angels, or merely material, such as the World, or lastly semi-spiritual and semi-corporeal, of an earthly and gross corporeity, such as man, so there may well be in existence a creature endowed with a rational spirit and a corporeity less gross, more subtle than man's. No doubt, moreover, but that after Resurrection, the souls of the blessed will be united with a glorious and subtle body; from which may be inferred that God may well have made a rational and corporeal creature whose body naturally enjoys the subtlety which will be conferred by the grace on the glorious body.

44.

But, the possible existence of such creatures will be still better set forth by solving the arguments which can be adduced against our conclusion, and replying to the questions it may raise.

45.

First question: should such creatures be styled rational animals?

And if so, in what do they differ from man, with whom they would have that definition in common?

46.

I reply: Yes, they would be rational animals, provided with senses and organs even as man; they would, however, differ from man not only in the more subtle nature, but also in the matter of their body. In fact, as is shown by Scripture, man has been made from the grossest of all elements, namely clay, a gross mixture of water and earth: but those creatures would be made from the most subtle part of all elements, or of one or other of them; thus, some would proceed from earth, others from water, or air, or fire; and, in order that they should not be defined in the same terms as man, to the definition of the latter should be added the mention of the gross materiality of his body, wherein he would differ from said animals.

47.

Second question: At" what period would those animals have been originated, and wherefrom? From earth, like the beasts, or from water, like quadrupeds, birds, etc.? Or, on the contrary, would they have been made, like man, by our Lord God?

48.

I reply: It is an article of belief, expressly laid down by the Council of Lateran, that whatever is in fact and at present, was made in the origin of the world. By His all-mighty virtue, God, from the beginning of time, raised together from nothing both orders of creatures, spiritual and corporeal. Now, those animals also would be included in the generality of creatures. As to their formation, it might be said that God Himself, through the medium of Angels, made their body as he did man's, to which an immortal spirit was to be united. That body being of a nobler nature than that of other animals, it was meet that it should be united to an incorporeal and highly noble spirit.

49.

Third question: Would those animals descend from one individual, as all men descend from Adam, or, on the contrary, would many have been made at the same time, as was the case for the other living things issued from earth and water, wherein were males and females for the preservation of the kind by generation? Would there be amongst them a distinction between the sexes? Would they be subject to birth and death, to senses, passions, want of food, power of growth? If so, what their nutrition? Would they lead a social life, as men do? By what laws ruled? Would they build up cities for their dwellings, cultivate the arts and sciences, hold property, and wage war between themselves, as men are wont to?

50.

I reply: It may be that all descend from one individual, as men descend from Adam; it may be also that a number of males and females were made initially, who preserved their kind by generation. ' We will further admit that they are born and die;. that they are divided into males and females, and are moved by senses and passions, as men are; that they feed and grow according to the size of their body; their food, however, instead of being gross like that required by the human body, must be delicate and vapoury, emanating through spirituous effluvia from whatever in the physical world abounds with highly volatile corpuscles, such as the flavour of meats, especially of roasts, the fume of wine, the fragrance of fruit, flowers, aromatics, which evolve an abundance of those effluvia until all their subtle and volatile parts have completely evaporated. To their being able to lead a social life, with distinctions of rank and precedence; to their cultivating the arts and sciences, exercising functions, maintaining armies, building up cities, doing in short whatever is requisite for their preservation, l have in the main no objection.

51.

Fourth question: What would their figure be, human or otherwise? Would the ordering of the divers parts of their body be essential, as with other animals, or merely accidental, as with fluid substances, such as oil, water, clouds, smoke, etc.? Would those organic parts consist of various substances, as is the case with the organs of the human body, wherein are to be found very gross parts, such as the bones, others less gross, such as the cartilages, and others slender, such as the membranes?

52.

l reply: As regards their figure, we neither can nor should be affirmative, since it escapes our senses, being too delicate for our sight or our touch. That we must leave to themselves, and to such as have the privilege of intuitive acquaintance with immaterial substances. But, so far as probability goes, I say that their figure tallies with the human body, save some distinctive peculiarity, should the very tenuity of their body not be deemed sufficient. I am led to that by the consideration that of all the works of God the human frame is the most perfect, and that whilst all other animals stoop to the ground, because their soul is mortal, God, as Ovid, the poet, says, in his *Metamorphoses*,

Gave man an erect figure, bidding him behold the heavens
And raise his face towards the stars,

man's soul having been made immortal for the heavenly abode. Considering that the animals we are speaking of Would be gifted with a spirit immaterial, rational and immortal, capable therefore of beatitude and damnation, it is proper to admit that the body to which that spirit is united may be like unto the most noble animal frame, that is to say to the human frame. Whence it follows that in the divers parts of that body there must be an essential order; that the foot, for instance, cannot be an appendage to the head, nor the hand to the belly, but that each organ is in its right place, according to the functions it has to perform. As to the constitutive parts of those organs, it is, in my opinion, necessary that there should be some more or less strong, others more or less slender, in order to meet the requirements of the organic working. Nor can this be fairly objected to on the ground of the slenderness of the bodies themselves; for the strength or thickness of the organic parts alluded to would not be absolute, but merely in comparison

with the more slender ones. That, moreover, may be observed in all
natural fluids, such as wine, oil, milk, etc.; however homogeneous
and similar to each other their component parts may look, yet they
are not so: for some are clayish, others aqueous; there are fixed
salts, volatile salts, brimstone, all of which are made obvious by a
chemical analysis. So it would be in our case: for, supposing the
bodies of those animals to be as subtle and slender as the natural
fluids, air, water, etc., there would nevertheless be discrepancies
in the quality of their constitutive parts, some of which would be
strong when compared with others more slender, although the
whole body which they compose might be called slender.

53.
It may be objected that this is repugnant to what was said above
concerning the essential ordering of the parts among themselves;
that it is seen that, in fluid and subtle bodies, one part is not
essentially but only accidentally connected with another; that a
part of wine, for instance, just now contiguous with some other,
soon comes in contact with a third, if the vessel be turned upside
down or the wine shaken, and that all the parts together exchange
positions at the same time, though it be still the same wine.
Whence it should be inferred that, the bodies of those animals
would have no permanent figure, and would consequently not be
organic.

54.
I reply that I deny the assumption. In fact, if in fluid bodies the

essential ordering of the parts is not apparent, it subsists none the less, and causes a compound to preserve its own state. Wine, for instance, when expressed from the grapes, seems a thoroughly homogeneous liquor, and yet is not so; for there are gross parts which, in the long run, subside in the casks; there are also slender parts which evaporate; fixed parts, such as tartar; volatile parts, such as brimstone and alcohol; others again, half volatile and half fixed, such as phlegm. Those divers parts do not respectively maintain an essential order; for no sooner has the must been expressed from the grapes, and been styled brimstone or volatile spirits, than it continues so closely involved with the particles of tartar, which is fixed, as not to be in any way able to escape.

55.

That is the reason why must recently expressed from the grapes is of no use for the distillation of the sulfurous spirits, commonly called *brandy*; but, after forty days fermentation, the particles of the wine change places: the spirits, no longer bound with the tartaric particles which they kept in suspension through their own volatility, whilst they were, in return, kept down by them and prevented from escaping, sever from those particles, and continue confused with the phlegmatic parts from which they become easily released by the operation of fire, and evaporate: thus, by means of distillation, brandy is made, which is nothing but the brimstone of wine volatilized by heat with the most slender part of phlegm. At the end of forty days another fermentation begins, which extends more or less, according as the maturity of the wine is more or less perfect, and the termination of which is dependent on the greater or lesser abundance of sulphurous spirits. If abounding with brimstone, the wine sours and turns to vinegar; if, on the contrary, it holds but little brimstone, it ropes, and becomes what the Italians call *vino molle or vino guasto*. If the wine is at once ripe, as happens in other cases, it sours or ropes in less time, as is shown by every day experience. Now, in said fermentation the essential order of the parts of wine is altered, but not so its quantity nor its matter, which neither changes nor decreases: a bottle that had been filled with wine is, after a certain time, found to be filled with vinegar, without any alteration in its quantity of matter; the essential order of its parts has alone been modified: the brimstone, which, as we have said, was united to the phlegm and separated from the tartar, becomes again involved and fixed with the tartar; so that, on distilling the vinegar, there issues from it first an insipid phlegm, and then spirits of vinegar, which are the brimstone of wine intermixed with particles of tartar that is less fixed. Now, the essential shifting of the aforesaid parts alters the substance of the juice of the grapes, as is clearly shown by the varied and contrary effects of must, wine, vinegar, and ropy or spoiled wine; for which cause the two first are fit, but the two last unfit materials for consecration. We have borrowed the above exposition of the economy of wine from the able work of Nicholas Lemery, perfumer to the King of France, *Course of Chemistry*, p. 2. c. q.

56.

If now we apply that natural doctrine to our subject, I say that, being given the corporeity of the animals in question, subtle and slender like the substance of liquids; being given also their organization and figure, which demand an essential order of the various parts, an adverse supposition could raise no argument contrary to their existence; for, just as the jumbling together of the parts of wine and the diversity of their accidental dispositions do not alter their essential order, even so it would be with the slender frame of our animals.

57.

Fifth question: Would those animals be subject to diseases and other infirmities under which mankind lies, such as ignorance, fear, idleness, sensual paralysis, etc.? Would they be wearied through labour, and require, for recruiting their strength, sleep, food, drink? And what food, what drink? Would they be fated to die, and might they be killed casually, or by the instrumentality of other animals?

58.

I reply: Their bodies, though subtle, being material, they would of course be liable to decay: they might therefore suffer from adverse agencies, and consequently be diseased; that is, their organs might not perform, or painfully and imperfectly perform the office assigned to them, for therein consist all diseases whatever with certain animals, as has been distinctly explained by the most illustrious Michael Ettmuller, *Physiology*, c. v. thesis i. In sooth, their body being less gross than the human frame, comprising less elements mixed together, and being therefore less composite, they would not so easily suffer from adverse influences, and would therefore be less liable to disease than man; their life would also exceed his; for, the more perfect an animal, as a species, the longer its days; thus mankind, whose existence extends beyond that of other animals. For I do not believe in the centenary existence of crows, stags, ravens and the like, of which Pliny tells his customary stories; and although his dreams have been reechoed by others without previous inquiry, it is no less clear that before writing thus, not one has faithfully noted the birth nor the death of those animals: they have been content with taking up the strange fable, as has been the case with the Phenix, whose longevity is discarded as a story by Tacitus, Annals, 6. It were therefore to be inferred that the animals we are speaking of would live longer still than man; for, as shall be said below, they would be more noble than he; consequently also, they would be subject to the other bodily affections, and require rest and food, as mentioned, number 50. Now, as rational beings amenable to discipline, they might also continue ignorant, if their minds did not receive the culture of study and instruction, and some amongst them would be more or less versed in science, more or less clever, according as their intelligence had been more or less trained. However, generally speaking, and considering the whole of the species, they would be more learned than men, not from the subtlety of their body, but perhaps because of the greater activity of their mind or the longer space of their life, which would enable them to learn more things than men: such are indeed the motives assigned by St. Augustine (Divin. Demon, ch. 3. and *Spirit and Soul*, ch. 37), to the prescience of the future in Demons. They might indeed suffer from natural agencies; but they could hardly be killed, on account of the speed with which they could escape from danger; it is therefore most unlikely that they could, without the greatest difficulty, be put to death or mutilated by beast or by man, with natural or artificial weapons, so quick would they be at avoiding the impending blow. Yet, they might be killed or mutilated in their sleep, or in a moment of inadvertence, by means of a solid body, such as a sword brandished by a man, or the fall of a heavy stone; for, although subtle, their body would be divisible, just like air which, though vaporous, is yet divided by a sword, a club, or any other solid body. Their spirit, however, would be indivisible, and like the human soul, entire in the whole and in each and every part of the body. Consequently, the division of their body by another body, as aforesaid, might occasion mutilation and even death, for the spirit, itself indivisible, could not animate both parts of a divided body. True, just as the parts of air, separated by the agency of a body, unite again as soon as that body is withdrawn, and constitute the same air as before, even so the parts of the body divided, as above-mentioned, might unite and be revived by the same spirit. But then, it must be inferred that those animals could not be slain by natural or artificial agencies: and it were more rational to keep to our first position; for, if sharing matter with other creatures, it is natural that they should be liable to suffer through those creatures, according to the common rule, and even unto death.

59.

Sixth question: Could their bodies penetrate other bodies, such as walls, wood, metals, glass, etc.? Could many of them abide together on the same material spot, and to what space would their body extend or be restrained?

60.

I reply: In all bodies, however compact, there are pores, as is apparent in metals where, more than in other bodies, it would seem there should be none; through a perfect microscope the pores of metals are discerned, with their different shapes. Now, those animals might, through the pores, creep into, and thus penetrate any other bodies, although such pores were impervious to other liquors or material spirits, of wine, ammoniacal salt, or the like, because their bodies would be much more subtle than those liquors. However, notwithstanding many Angels may abide together on the same material spot, and even confine themselves in a lesser and lesser space, though not infinitely, as is shown by Scott, yet it were rash to ascribe the same power to those animals; for, their bodies are determined in substance and impervious to each other; and if two glorious bodies cannot abide together on the same spot, though a glorious and a non glorious one may do so, according to some Doctors, much less would it be possible for the bodies of those animals, which are indeed subtle, yet do not attain to the subtlety of the glorious body. As regards their power of extension or compression, we may instance the case of air, which, rarefied and condensed, occupies more or less room, and may even, by artificial means, be compressed into a narrower space than would be naturally due to its volume; as is seen with those large balls which, for amusement, one inflates by means of a blow-pipe or tube: air, being forced into them and compressed, is held in larger quantity than is warranted by the capacity of the ball. Similarly the bodies of the animals we are speaking of might, by their natural virtue, extend to a larger space, not exceeding however their own substance; they might also contract, but not beyond the determined space due to that same substance. And, considering that of their number, as with men, some would be tall and some short, it were proper that the tall should be able to extend more than the short, and the short to contract more than the tall.

61.

Seventh question: Would those animals be born in original sin, and have been redeemed by the Lord Christ? Would the grace have been conferred upon them and through what sacraments? Under what law would they live, and would they be capable of beatitude and damnation?

62.

I reply: It is an article of belief that Christ has merited grace and glory for all rational creatures without exception. It is also an article of belief that glory is not conferred on a rational creature until such creature has been previously endowed with grace, which is the disposition to glory. According to a like article, glory is conferred but by merits. Now, those merits are grounded on the perfect observance of the commands of God, which is accomplished through grace. The above questions are thus solved. Whether those creatures did or did not sin originally is uncertain. It is clear, however, that if their first Parent had sinned as Adam sinned, his descent would be born in original sin, as men are born. And, as God never leaves a rational creature without a remedy, so long as it treads the way, if those creatures were infected with original or with actual sin, God would have provided them with a remedy; but whether it is the case, and of what kind is the remedy, is a secret between God and them. Surely, if they had sacraments identical with or different from those in use in the human Church militant, for the institution and efficacy thereof they would be indebted to the merits of Jesus Christ, the Redeemer and universal Atoner of all rational creatures. It would likewise be highly proper, nay necessary, that they should live under some law given them by God, and through the observance of which they might merit beatitude; but what would be that law, whether merely natural or written, Mosaic or Evangelical, or different from all these and specially instituted by God, that we are ignorant of. Whatever it might be though, there would follow no objection exclusive of the possible existence of such creatures.

63.

The only argument, and that a rather lame one, which long meditations has suggested to me against the possibility of such creatures, is that, if they really existed in the World, we should find them mentioned somewhere by Philosophers, Holy Scripture, Ecclesiastical Tradition, or the Holy Fathers: such not being the case, their utter impossibility should be inferred.

64.

But that argument which, in fact, calls in question their existence rather than their possibility, is easily disposed of by our premises, Ns. 41 and 42; for no argument can stand in virtue of a negative authority. Besides, it is not correct to assert that neither the Philosophers, nor the Scriptures, nor the Fathers have handed down any notion of them. Plato, as is reported by Apuleius (*The Demon of Socrates*) and Plutarch (*Isis and Osiris*), declared that Demons were beings of the animal kind, passive souls, rational intelligences, aerial bodies, everlasting; and he gave them the name of *Demons*, which of itself is nowise offensive, since it means *replete with wisdom*; so that, when authors allude to the Devil (*or Evil Angel*), they do not merely call him Demon, but *Cacodemon*, and say likewise *Eudemon*, when speaking of a good Angel. Those creatures are also mentioned in Scripture and by the Fathers, as shall be said hereafter.

65.

Now that we have proved that those creatures are possible, let us go a step further, and show that they exist. Taking for granted the truth of the recitals concerning the intercourse of Incubi and Succubi with men and beasts, recitals so numerous that it would look like impudence to deny the fact, as is said by St Austin, whose testimony is given above (Nr 10), I argue: Where the peculiar passion of the sense is found, there also, of necessity, is the sense itself; for, according to the principles of philosophy, the peculiar passion flows from nature, that is to say: that, where the acts and operations of the sense are found, there also is the sense, the operations and acts being but its external form. Now, those, Incubi and Succubi present acts, operations, peculiar passions, which spring from the senses; they are therefore endowed with, senses. But senses cannot exist without concomitant composite organs, without a combination of soul and body. Incubi and Succubi have therefore body and soul, and, consequentially, are animals; but their acts and operations are also those of a rational soul; their soul is therefore rational; and thus, from first to last, they are rational animals.

66.
Our minor is easy of demonstration in each of its parts. And indeed, the appetitive passion of coition is a sensual passion; the grief, sadness, wrath, rage, occasioned by the denial of coition, are sensual passions, as is seen with all animals; generation through coition is evidently a sensual operation. Now, all that happens with Incubi, as has been shown above: they incite women, sometimes even men; if denied, they sadden and storm, like lovers: *amantes, amentes*; they perfectly practice coition, and sometimes beget. It must therefore be inferred that they have senses, and consequently a body; consequently also, that they are perfect animals. More than that: with closed doors and windows they

enter wherever they please: their body is therefore slender; they foreknow and foretell the future, compose and divide, all which operations arc proper to a rational soul; they therefore possess a rational soul and are, in sooth, rational animals.

Doctors generally retort that it is the Evil Spirit that perpetrates those impure acts, simulates passions, love, grief at the denial of coition, in order to entice souls to sin and to undo them; and that, if he copulates and begets, it is with assumed sperm and body, as aforesaid (Nr 24).

67.

But then, there are Incubi that have to do with horses, mares and other beasts, and, as shown by every day experience, illtreat them if rebel to coition; yet, in those cases, it can no longer be adduced that the Demon simulates the appetite for coition in order to bring about the ruin of souls, since those of beasts are not capable of everlasting damnation. Besides, love and wrath with them are productive of quite opposite effects. For, if the loved woman or beast humours them, those Incubi behave very well; on the contrary, they use them most savagely when irritated and enraged by a denial of coition: this is amply proved by daily experience: those Incubi therefore have truly sexual passions. Besides, the Evil Spirits, the incorporeal Demons which have to do with Sorceresses and Witches, constrain them to Demon- Worship, to the abjuration of the Orthodox Faith, to the commission of enchantments and foul crimes, as preliminary conditions to the infamous intercourse, as has been above-stated (Nr 11); now, Incubi pretend to nothing of the kind: they are therefore no Evil Spirits. Lastly, as written by Guaccius, at the mere utterance of the name of Jesus or Mary, at the sign of the Cross, the approach of Holy Relics or consecrated objects, at exorcisms, adjurations or priestly injunctions, the Evil Demon either shudders and takes to flight, or is agitated and howls, as is daily seen with energumens and is shown by numerous narratives of Guaccius concerning the nightly revels of Witches, where, at a sign of the Cross or the name of Jesus said by one of the assistants. Devils and Witches all vanish together. Incubi, on the contrary, stand all those ordeals without taking to flight or showing the least fear; sometimes even they laugh at exorcisms, strike the Exorcists themselves, and rend the sacred vestments. Now, if the evil Demons, subdued by our Lord Jesus-Christ, are stricken with fear by his name, the Cross and the holy things; if, on the other hand, the good Angels rejoice at those same things, without however inciting men to sin nor to give offense to God, whilst the Incubi, without having any dread of the holy things, provoke to sin, it is clear that they are neither evil Demons nor good Angels; but it is clear also that they are not men, though endowed with reason. What then should they be? Supposing them to have reached the goal, and to be pure spirits, they would be damned or blessed, for correct Theology does not admit of pure spirits on the way to salvation. If damned, they would revere the name and the Cross of Christ; if blessed, they would not incite men to sin; they would therefore be different from pure spirits, and thiis, have a body and be on the way to salvation.

68.

Besides, a material agent cannot act but on an equally material passive. It is indeed a trite philosophical axiom, that agent and patient must have a common subject: pure matter cannot act on any purely spiritual thing. Now, there are natural agents which act on those Incubi Demons: these are therefore material or corporeal. Our minor is proved by the testimony of Dioscorides, Pliny, Aristoteles and Apuleius, quoted by Guaccius, *Comp. Malef.* b. 3, ch. 13, fol. 316; it is confirmed by our knowledge of numerous herbs, stones and animal substances which have the virtue of driving away Demons, such as rue, St-John's wort, verbena, germander, palma Christi, centaury, diamonds, coral, jet, jasper, the skin of the head of a wolf or an ass, women's catamenia, and a hundred others: wherefore it is written: *For such as are assaulted by the Demon it is lawful to have stones or herbs, but without recourse to incantations.* It follows that, by their own native virtue, stones or herbs can bridle the Demon: else the above mentioned Canon would not permit their use, but would on the contrary forbid it as superstitious. We have a striking instance thereof in Holy Scripture, where the Angel Raphael says to Tobit, ch. 6, v. 8, speaking of the fish which he had drawn from the Tigris: "*If thou puttest on coals a particle of its liver, the smoke thereof will drive away all kinds of Demons.*" Experience demonstrated the truth those words'; for, no sooner was the liver of the fish set on fire, than the Incubus who was in love with Sarah was put to flight.

69.

To this Theologians usually retort that such natural agents merely initiate the ejection of the Demon, and that the completive effect is due to the supernatural force of God or of the Angel; so that the supernatural force is the primary, direct and principal cause, the natural force being but secondary, indirect and subordinate. Thus, in order to explain how the liver ot the fish burnt by Tobit drove away the Demon, Vallesius asserts that the smoke thereof had been endowed by God with the supernatural power of expelling the Incubus, in the same manner as the material fire of Hell has the virtue of tormenting Demons and the souls of the Damned. Others, such as Lyranus and Cornelius, profess that the smoke of the heart of the fish initiated the ejection of the Demon by native virtue, but completed it by angelical and heavenly virtue: by native virtue, insomuch that it opposed a contrary action to that of the Demon; for the Evil Spirit applies native causes and humours, the native qualities of which are combated by the contrary qualities of natural things known to be capable of driving away Demons; that opinion is shared by all those who treat of the art of exorcisms.

70.

But that explanation, however plausible the facts upon which it rests, can at most be received as regards the Evil Spirits which possess bodies or, through malefice, infect them with diseases or other infirmities; it does not at all meet the case of Incubi. For, these neither possess bodies nor infect them with diseases; they, at most, molest them by blows and ill-treatment. If they cause the

mares to grow lean because of their not yielding to coition, it is
merely by taking away their provender, in consequence of which
they fall off and finally die. To that purpose the Incubus need
not use a natural agent, as the Evil Spirit does when imparting a
disease: it is enough that it should exert its own native organic
force. Likewise, when the Evil Spirit possesses bodies and infects
them with diseases, it is most frequently through signs agreed
upon with himself, and arranged by a witch or a wizard, which
signs are usually natural objects, imbued with their own noxious
virtue, and of course opposed by other equally natural objects
endowed with a contrary virtue. But not so the Incubus: it is of his
own accord, and without the cooperation of either witch or wizard,
that he inflicts his molestations. Besides, the natural things which
put the Incubi to flight exert their virtue and bring about a result
without the intervention of any exorcism or blessing; it cannot
therefore be said that the ejection of the Incubus is initiated by
natural, and completed by divine virtue, since there is in this case
no particular invocation of the divine name, but the mere effect
of a natural object, in which God cooperates only as the universal
agent, the author of nature, the first of efficient causes.

71.

To illustrate this subject, I give two stories, the first of which I have
from a Confessor of Nuns, a man of weight, and most worthy of
credit; the second I was eye-witness to. In a certain monastery
of holy Nuns there lived, as a boarder, a young maiden of noble
birth, who was tempted by an Incubus that appeared to her by day

and by night and with the most earnest entreaties, the manners
of a most passionate lover, incessantly incited her to sin; but
she, supported by the grace of God and the frequent use of the
sacraments, stoutly resisted the temptation. But, all her devotions,
fasts and vows notwithstanding, despite the exorcisms, the
blessings, the injunctions showered by exorcists on the Incubus
that he should desist from molesting her; in spite of the crowd of
relics and other holy objects collected in the maiden's room, of
the lighted candles kept burning there all night, the Incubus none
the less persisted in appearing to her as usual, in the shape of a
very handsome young man. At last, among other learned men,
whose advice had been taken on the subject, was a very erudite
Theologian who, observing that the maiden was of a thoroughly
phlegmatic temperament, surmised that that Incubus was an
aqueous Demon (there are in fact, as is testified by Guaccius,
igneus aerial, phlegmatic, earthly, subterranean demons who avoid
the light of day), and prescribed an uninterrupted fumigation in
the room. A new vessel, made of glass-like earth, was accordingly
brought in, and filled with sweet cane, cubeb seed, roots of both
aristolochies, great and small cardamon, ginger, long-pepper,
caryophylleae, cinnamon, cloves, mace, nutmegs, calamite storax,
benzoin, aloes-wood and roots, one ounce of triasandalis, and
three pounds of half brandy and water; the vessel was then set
on hot ashes in order to force up the fumigating vapour, and the
cell was kept closed. As soon as the fumigation was done, the
Incubus came, but never dared enter the cell; only, if the maiden
left it for a walk in the garden or the cloister, he appeared to her,

though invisible to others and throwing his arms round her neck, stole or rather snatched kisses from her, to her intense disgust. At last, after a new consultation, the Theologian prescribed that she should carry about her person pills made of the most exquisite perfumes, such as musk, amber, chive, Peruvian balsam, and others. Thus provided, she went for a walk in the garden, where the Incubus suddenly appeared to her with a threatening face, and in a rage. He did not approach her, however, but, after biting his finger as if meditating revenge, disappeared and was never more seen by her.

72.

Here is the other story. In the great Carthusian Friary of Pavia there lived a Deacon, Austin by name, who was subjected by a certain Demon to excessive, unheard of and scarcely credible vexations; although many exorcists had made repeated endeavours to secure his riddance, all spiritual remedies had proved unavailing. I was consulted by the Vicar of the convent, who had the cure of the poor clerk. Seeing the inefficacy of all customary exorcisms, and remembering the above-related instance, I advised a fumigation like unto the one that has been detailed, and prescribed that the Deacon should carry about his person fragrant pills of the same kind; moreover, as he was in the habit of using tobacco, and was very fond of brandy, I advised tobacco and brandy perfumed with musk. The Demon appeared to him by day and by night, under various shapes, as a skeleton, a pig, an ass, an Angel, a bird; with the figure of one or other of the Friars, once even with that of his own Abbot or Prior, exhorting him to keep his conscience clean, to trust in God, to confess frequently; he persuaded him to let him hear his sacramental confession, recited with him the psalms *Exsurgat Deus and Qui habitat*, and the Gospel according to St. John: and when they came to the words *Verbum carofactum est*, he bent his knee, and taking hold of a stole which was in the cell, and of the Holy-water sprinkle, he blessed the cell and the bed," and, as if he had really been the Prior, enjoined on the Demon not to venture in future to molest his subordinate; he then disappeared, thus betraying what he was, for otherwise the young deacon had taken him for his Prior. Now, notwithstanding the fumigations and perfumes I had prescribed, the Demon did not desist from his wonted apparitions; more than that, assuming the features of his victim, he went to the Vicar's room, and asked for some tobacco and brandy perfumed with musk, of which, said he, he was extremely fond. Having received both, he disappeared in the twinkling of an eye, thus showing the Vicar that he had been played with by the Demon; and this was amply confirmed by the Deacon, who affirmed upon his oath that he had not gone that day to the Vicar's cell. All that having been related to me, I inferred that, far from being aqueous like the Incubus who was in love with the maiden above spoken of, this Demon was igneous, or, at the very least, aerial, since he delighted in hot substances such as vapours, perfumes, tobacco and brandy. Force was added to my surmises by the temperament of the young deacon, which was choleric and sanguine, choler predominating however; for, those Demons never approach but those whose temperament tallies with their own: another confirmation of my sentiment regarding their corporeity. I therefore advised the Vicar to let his penitent take herbs that are cold by nature, such as water-lily, liver-wort, spurge, mandrake, house-leek, plantain, henbane, and others similar, make two little bundles of them and hang them up, one at his window, the other at the door of his cell, taking care to strew some also on the floor and on the bed. Marvelous to say! The Demon appeared again, but remained outside the room, which he would not enter; and, on the Deacon inquiring of him his motives for such unwonted reserve, he burst out into invectives against me for giving such advice, disappeared, and never came again.

73.

The two stories I have related make it clear that, by their native virtue alone, perfumes and herbs drove away Demons without the intervention of any supernatural force; Incubi are therefore subject to, material conditions, and it must be inferred that they participate of the matter of the natural objects which have the power of putting them to flight, and consequently they have a body; that is what was to be shown.

74.

But, the better to establish our conclusion, it behooves to impugn the mistake into which have fallen the Doctors above quoted, such as Vallesius and Cornelius a Lapide, when they say that Sarah was rid from the Incubus by the virtue of the Angel Raphael, and not by that of the callionymous fish caught by Tobit on the banks of the Tigris. Indeed, saving the reverence due to such great doctors, such a construction manifestly clashes with the clear meaning of the Text, from which it is never justifiable to deviate, so long as it does not lead to absurd consequences. Here are the words spoken by the Angel to Tobias: *"If thou puttest on coals a particle of its heart, the smoke thereof will expel all kinds of Demons, whether from man or woman, so that they shall never return, and it's gall is good for anointing eyes, that have whiteness, and healing them."* (Tobit, c. 6, v. 8 and 9). Pray notice that the Angel's assertion respecting the virtue of the heart or liver and gall of that fish is absolute, universal; for, he does not say: *"If thou puttest on coals particles of its heart, thou wilt put to flight all kinds of Demons, and if thou anointest with its gall eyes that have a whiteness, they shall be healed."* If he had thus spoken, I could agree with the construction that Raphael had brought about, by his own supernatural virtue, the effects which the mere application of the smoke and the gall might not have sufficed to produce: but he does not speak thus, and, on the contrary, says absolutely, that such is the virtue of the smoke and the gall.

75.

It may be asked whether the Angel spoke the precise truth regarding the virtue of those things, or whether he might have lied; and likewise, whether the whiteness was withdrawn from the eyes of the elder Tobit by the native force of the gall of the fish, or by the supernatural virtue of the Angel Raphael? To say that the Angel could have lied would be an heretical blasphemy; he therefore spoke the precise truth; but it would no longer be so if all kinds of Demons were not expelled by the smoke of the liver of the fish, unless aided by the supernatural force of the Angel, and especially, if such aid was the principal cause of the effect produced, as the Doctors assert in the present case. It would doubtless be a lie if a physician should say: such an herb radically cures pleurisy or epilepsy, and if it should only begin the cure, the completion of which required the addition of another herb to the one first used; in the same manner, Raphael would have lied when averring that the smoke of the liver expelled all kinds of demons, so that they should not return, if that result had been only begun by the smoke, audits completion had been principally due to the virtue of the Angel. Besides, that flight of the demon was either to take place universally and by any one whomsoever putting the liver of the fish on the coals, or else it was only to occur in that particular case, the younger Tobit putting the liver on. In the first hypothesis, any person making that smoke by burning the liver should be assisted by an Angel, who, through his supernatural virtue should expel the Demons miraculously and regularly at the same time; which is absurd; for, either words have no meaning, or a natural fact cannot be regularly followed by a miracle, and, if the Demon was not put to flight without the assistance of the Angel, Raphael would have lied when ascribing that virtue to the liver. If, on the contrary, that effect was only to be brought about in that particular case, Raphael would again have lied when assigning to that fish, universally and absolutely, the virtue of expelling the Demon: now, to say that the Angel lied is not possible.

76.

The whiteness was withdrawn from the eyes of the elder Tobit, and his blindness healed, through the native virtue of the gall of that same fish, as Doctors aver. In fact, that the gall of the callionymous fish, which the Italians call *bocca in capo*, and of which Tobias made use, is a highly renowned remedy for removing the whiteness from the eyes, all are agreed, Dioscorides, Galen, Pliny, Aclanius, Vallesius, etc. The Greek Text of *Tobit*, c. 11, v. i3, says: "*He poured the gall on his father 's eyes, saying: Have confidence, father; but, there being erosion, the old man rubbed his eyes, and the scales of the whiteness came out at the corners.*" Now, since, according to the same text, the Angel had disclosed to Tobias the virtue of the liver and gall of the fish, and since, through its native virtue, the gall cured the elder Tobit 's blindness, it must be inferred that it was likewise through its native force that the smoke of the liver put the Incubus to flight; which inference is conclusively confirmed by the Greek text, which, Tobit, c 8, v. 2, instead of the reading in the Vulgate: "*He laid a part of the liver on burning coals*", says explicitly: "*He took the ashes of the perfumes, and put the heart and the liver of the fish thereupon, and made a smoke therewith; the which smell when the evil spirit had smelled, he fled.*" The Hebrew text says: "*Asmodeus smelled the smell, and fled.*" From all those texts it appears that the Demon took to flight on smelling a smoke which was prejudicial and hurtful to himself, and nowise from the supernatural virtue of the Angel. If, in, ridding Sarah from the assaults of the Incubus Asmodeus, the operation of the smoke of the liver was followed by the intervention of Raphael, it was in order to bind the Demon in the wilderness of High-Egypt, as related, *Tobit.*, c. 8, v. 3; for, at such a distance, the smoke of the liver could neither operate on the Demon, nor bind him. And here we have the means of reconciling our opinion with that of the above-mentioned Doctors, who ascribe to Raphael's power Sarah's complete riddance from the Demon: for, I say with them, that the cure of Sarah was completed by the binding of the Demon in the wilderness, the deed of the Angel; which I concede; but I maintain that the deliverance properly called, that is to say, the ejection from Sarah's bed-room, was the direct effect of the virtue of the liver of the fish.

77.

A third principal proof of our con. elusion regarding the existence of those animals, in other words, respecting the corporeity of Incubi, is adduced by the testimony of St Hieronymus, in his *Life of St Paul, the first Hermit.* St Anthony, says he, set on a journey to visit St Paul. After travelling several days, he met a Centaur, of whom he inquired the hermit's abode; whereupon the Centaur answered growling some uncouth and scarcely intelligible, showed the way with his out-stretched hand, and fled with the utmost speed into a wood. The Holy Abbot kept on his way, and, in a dale, met a little man, almost a dwarf, with crooked hands, horned brow, and his lower extremities ending with goat's feet. At the sight of him, St Anthony stood still, and fearing the arts of the Devil, comforted himself with a sign of the Cross. But, far from running away, or even seeming frightened at it, the little fellow respectfully approached the old man, and tendered him, as a peace offering, dates for his journey. The blessed St Anthony having then inquired who he was: *"I am a mortal," replied he, "and one of the inhabitants of the Wilderness, whom Gentility, under its varied delusions, worships under the names of Fauns, Satyrs and Incubi; I am on a mission from my flock: we request thee to pray for us unto the common God, whom we know to have come for the salvation of the world, and whose praises are sounded all over the earth."* Rejoicing at the glory of Christ, St Anthony, turning his face towards Alexandria, and striking the ground with his staff, cried out: *"Woe be unto thee, thou harlot City, who worshipest animals as Gods!"* Such is the narrative of St Hieronymus, who expatiates at length on the fact, explaining its import in along discourse.

78.

It were indeed rash to doubt the truth of the above recital, constantly referred to by the greatest of the Doctors of the Holy Church, St Hieronymus, whose authority no Catholic will ever deny. Let us therefore investigate the circumstances thereof which most clearly confirm our opinion.

79.

Firstly, we must observe that if ever a Saint was assailed by the arts of the Demon, saw through his infernal devices, and carried off victories and trophies from the contest, that Saint was St Anthony, as is shown by his life written by St Aihanasius. Now, since in that little man St Anthony did not recognize a devil but an animal, saying: *"Woe be unto thee, thou harlot City, who worshipest animals as Gods!"*, it is clear that it was no devil or pure spirit ejected from heaven and damned, but some kind of animal. Still more: St Anthony, when instructing his friars and cautioning them against the assaults of the Demon, said to them, as related in the Roman Breviary (*Festival of St Anthony, Abbot, b. I*): *"Believe me, my brethren, Satan dreads the vigils of pious men, their prayers, fasts, voluntary poverty, compassion and humility; but, above all, he dreads their burning love of our Lord Christ, at the mere sign of whose most Holy Cross he flies disabled."* As the little man, against whom St Anthony guarded himself with a sign of the Cross, neither took fright nor fled, but approached the Saint confidently and humbly, offering him some dates, it is a sure sign that he was no Devil.

80.

Secondly, we must observe that the little man said: *"I also am a mortal"*, whence it follows that he was an animal subject to death, and consequently called into being through generation; for, an immaterial spirit is immortal, because simple, and consequently is not called into being through generation from preexistent matter, but through creation, and, consequently also, cannot lose it through the corruption called death; its existence can only come to an end through annihilation. Therefore, when saying he was mortal, he professed himself an animal.

81.

Thirdly, we must observe that he said he knew that the common God had suffered in human flesh. Those words show him to have been a rational animal, for brutes know nothing but what is sensible and present, and can therefore have no knowledge of God. If that little man said that he and his fellows were aware of God having suffered in human flesh, it shows that, by means of some revelation, he had acquired the notion of God, as we have ourselves the revealed faith. That God assumed human flesh and suffered in it, is the essence of the two principal articles of our Faith; the existence of God one and threefold, His Incarnation, Passion and Resurrection. All that shows, as I said, that it was a rational animal, capable of the knowledge of God through revelation, like ourselves, and endowed with a rational, and consequently, immortal soul.

82.

Fourthly, we must observe that, in the name of his whole flock whose delegate he professed to be, he besought St Anthony to pray for them to the common God. Wherefrom I infer that that little man was capable of beatitude and damnation, and that he was not *in termino* but *in via*; for, from his being, as has been shown above, rational and consequently endowed with an immortal soul, it flows that he was capable of beatitude and damnation, the proper share of every rational Creature, Angel or man. I likewise infer that he was on the way, *in via*, that is, capable of merit and demerit; for, if he had been at the goal, *in termino*, he would have been either blessed or damned. Now, he could be neither the one nor the other; for, St Anthony's prayers, to which he commended himself, could have been of no assistance to him, if finally damned, and, if blessed, he stood in no need of them. Since he commended himself to those prayers, it shows they could be of avail to him, and, consequently, that he was on the way to salvation, *in statu vice et meriti*.

83.

Fifthly, we must observe that the little man professed to be delegated by others of his kind, when saying: *"I am on a mission from myflock"*, words from which many inferences may be deduced. One is, that the little man was not alone of his kind, an exceptional and solitary monster, but that there were many of the same species, since congregating they made up a flock, and that he came in the name of all; which could not have been, had not the will of many centered in him. Another is, that those animals lead a social life, since one of them was sent in the name of many. Another again is, that, although living in the Wilderness, it is not assigned to them as a permanent abode; for St Anthony having never previously been in that desert, which was far distant from his hermitage, they could not have known who he was nor what his degree of sanctity; it was therefore necessary that they should have become acquainted with him elsewhere, and, consequently, that they should have travelled beyond that wilderness.

84.

Lastly, we must observe that the little man said he was one of those whom *the Gentiles, blinded by error, call Fauns, Satyrs and Incubi*: and by these words is shown the truth of our principal proposition: that Incubi are rational animals, capable of beatitude and damnation.

85.

The apparition of such little men is of frequent occurrence in metallic mines, as is written by Gregorius Agricola in his book *De Animal, subterran.* They appear to the miners, clothed like themselves, play and caper together, laugh and titter, and throw little stones at them for the sake of amusement: a sign, says the above named Author, of excellent success, and of the finding of some branch or body of a mineral tree.

86.

Peter Thyraeus, of Neuss, in his book *De Terrification. nocturn.*, denies the existence of such little men, and supports his denial upon the following truly puerile arguments: given such little men, says he, where do they live, how and where do they dwell? How do they keep up their kind, through generation or otherwise? Are they born, do they die, with what food do they sustain themselves? Are they capable of beatitude and damnation, and by what means do they procure their salvation? Such are the arguments upon which Thyrseus relies for denying that existence.

87.

But it really shows little judgment in a man, to deny that which has been written by grave and credible Authors, and confirmed by every day experience. Thyreus' arguments are worthless and have been already refuted, Nos. 45 and following. The only question which remains to be answered is this: where do those little men, or Incubi, dwell? To that I reply: as has been shown above (No 71), according to Guaccius, some are earthly, some aqueous, some aerial, some igneous, that is to say, that their bodies are made of the most subtle part of one of the elements, or, if of the combination of many elements, that yet there is one which predominates, either water or air, according to their nature. Their dwellings will consequently be found in that element which is prevalent in their bodies: igneous Incubi, for instance, will only stay forcibly, may be will not stay at all, in water or marshes, which are adverse to them; and aqueous Incubi will not be able to rise into the upper part of ether, the subtlety of which region is repugnant to them. We see the like happen to men who, accustomed to thicker air, cannot reach certain lofty ridges of the Alps where the air is too subtle for their lungs.

88.

Many testimonies of Holy Fathers, gathered by Molina, in his *Commentary of St. Thomas*, would go to prove the corporeity of Demons; but, taking into account the above-quoted decision of the Council of Lateran (No 37), concerning the incorporeity of Angels, we must understand that the Holy Fathers had in view those Incubi

Demons which are still on the way to salvation, and not those that are damned. However, to make matters short, we merely give the authority of St Augustine, that eminent Doctor of the Church, and it will be clearly seen how thoroughly his doctrine harmonizes with ours.

89.

St Augustine, then, in his *Commentary on Genesis*, book 2, ch. 17, writes as follows concerning Demons: "*They have the knowledge of some truths, partly through the more subtle acumen of their senses, partly through the greater subtlety of their bodies*", and, book 3, ch. i: "*Demons are aerial animals, because they partake of the nature of aerial bodies.*" In his Epistle ii5 to Hebridius, he affirms that they are "*aerial or ethereal animals, endowed with very sharp senses*". In the *City of God*, book ll, ch. 13, he says that "*the worst Demon has an aerial body*". Book 21, ch. 10, he writes: "*The bodies of certain Demons., as has been believed by some learned men, are even made of the thick and damp air which we breathe.*" Book 15, ch. 23: "*He dares not define whether Angels, with an aerial body, could feel the lust which would incite them to communicate with women.*" In his commentary on Psalm 85, he says that "*the bodies of the blessed will, after resurrection, be like unto the bodies of Angels;*" Psalm 14, he observes that "*the body of Angels is inferior to the soul.*" And, in his book *De Divinit. Dæmonum*, he everywhere, and especially ch. 23, teaches that "*Demons have subtle bodies*".

90.

Our doctrine can also be confirmed by the testimony of the Holy Scriptures, which, however diversely construed by commentators, are yet capable of adaptation to our proposition. First, Psalm 77, v. 24 and 2 5, it is said: *"The Lord had given them of the bread of heaven; man did eat angels' food."* David here alludes to Manna, which fed the People of Israel during the whole time that they wandered in the wilderness. It will be asked in what sense it can be said of Manna that it is the *Bread of Angels.* I am aware that most Doctors construe this passage in a mystical sense, saying that Manna figures the Holy Eucharist, which is styled the bread of Angels, because Angels enjoy the sight of God who, by concomitance, is found in the Eucharist.

91.

A most proper construction assuredly, and which is adopted by the Church in the office of the *Most Holy Body of Jesus Christ*; but it is in a spiritual sense. Now, what I want, is the literal sense; for, in that Psalm, David does not speak, as a prophet, of things to be, as he does in other places where a literal sense is not easily to be gathered; he speaks here as a historian, of things gone by. That Psalm, as is evident to whoever reads it, is a pure anacephalæosis, or summing up of all the benefits conferred by God on the Hebrew People from the exodus from Egypt to the days of David, and the Manna of the Wilderness is spoken of in it; how, and in what sense is it styled the Bread of Angels? that is the question.

92.

I am aware that others look upon the Bread of Angels as bread prepared by Angels, or sent down from Heaven by the ministry of Angels. But Cardinal Hugo explains that qualification by saying that that food partly produced the same effect upon the Jews, which the food of Angels produces upon the latter. Angels, in fact, are not liable to any infirmity; on the other hand Hebrew commentators, and Josephus himself, assert that whilst in the Wilderness, living upon Manna, the Jews' neither grew old, nor sickened, nor tired; so that Manna was like unto the bread that Angels feed upon, who know neither old age, nor sickness, nor fatigue.

93.

These interpretations should indeed be received with the respect due to the authority of such eminent Doctors. There is however one difficulty in this: that, by the ministry of Angels, the pillars of the cloud and fire, the quails, and the water from the rock were provided for the Hebrews, no less than the Manna; and yet they were not styled the pillar, the water or the beverage of Angels. Why therefore should Manna be called *Bread of Angels*, because provided by their ministry, when the qualification *Beverage of Angels* is not given to the water drawn from the rock likewise by their ministry? Besides, in Holy Scripture, when it is said of bread that it is the *bread of somebody*, it is always the bread of him who feeds on it, not of him who provides or makes it. Of this there are numberless instances: thus. *Exodus*, ch. 23, V. 25: *"That I may bless thy bread and thy water;"* Kings, book 2, ch. 12,

v. 3: "*Eating of his bread,*" Tobit, ch. 4, v. 17: "*Give of thy bread to the hungry,*" and V. 18: "*Pour out thy bread on the burial of the Just*; "Ecclesiasticus, ch. 11, V. l: "*Scatter thy bread over the flowing waters,* "Isaiah, ch. 58, v. 7: "*Deal thy bread to the hungry,* "Jeremiah, ch. 11, V. 19: "*Let us put wood into his bread,*" Matthew, ch. i.5, v. 26: "*It is not meet to take the children's bread,*" Luke, ch. 11, V. 3: "*Our daily bread.*" All those passages clearly show that, in Scripture, the bread of somebody is the bread of him who feeds upon it, not of him who makes, brings or provides it. In the passage of the Psalm we have quoted, *Bread of Angels* may therefore easily be taken to mean the food of Angels, not incorporeal indeed, since these require no material food, but corporeal, that is to say of those rational animals we have discoursed of, who live in the air, and, from the subtlety of their bodies and their rationality, approximate so closely to immaterial Angels as to fall under the same denomination.

94.

I deduce that, being animals, consequently reproducible through generation and liable to corruption, they require food for the restoration of their corporeal substance wasted by effluvia: for the life of every sensible being consists in nothing else but the motion of the corporeal elements which flow and ebb, are acquired, lost and recruited by means of substances spirituous, yet material, assimilated by the living thing, either through the inhalation of air, or by the fermentation of food which spiritualizes its substance, as shown by the most learned Ettmuller (*Instit. Medic. Physiolog.*, ch. 2).

95.

But, their body being subtle, equally subtle and delicate must be
its food. And, just as perfumes and other vaporous and volatile
substances, when adverse to their nature, offend and put them
to flight, as testified by what we related above (Nos. 71 and 72),
in the like manner, when agreeable, they delight in and feed upon
them. Now, as is written by Cornelius, *"Manna is nothing but an
emanation of water and earth, refined and baked by the heat of
the sun, and then coagulated and condensed by the cold of the
following night,"* of course, I am speaking of the Manna sent down
from Heaven for the nourishment of the Hebrews, and which
differs all in ail from nostrate or medicinal manna: the latter, in
fact, according to Ettmuller (*Dilucid. Physiol.*, ch. i), *"is merely
the juice or transudation of certain trees which, during the night,
gets mixed up with dew, and, the next morning, coagulates and
thickens in the heat of the sun."* The manna of the Hebrews, on
the contrary, derived from other principles, far from coagulating,
liquefied in the heat of the sun, as is shown by Scripture, Exodus,
ch. 16, v. 22. The manna of the Hebrews was therefore undoubtedly
of a most subtle substance, consisting as it did of emanations
of earth and water, and being dissolved by the sun and made to
disappear: consequently, it may very well have been the food of
the animals we are speaking of, and thus have been truly called by
David *Bread of Angels*.

96.

We have another authority in the Gospel according to St. John, ch.

10, v. 16, where it is said: "*And other sheep I have, which are not of this fold: them also I must bring, and they shall hear my voice, and there shall be one fold and one shepherd.*" If we inquire what are those sheep which are not of that fold, and what the fold of which the Lord Christ speaketh, we are answered by all Commentators that the only fold of Christ is the Church to which the preaching of the Gospel was to bring the Gentiles, sheep of another fold than that of the Hebrews. They are, in fact, of opinion that the fold of Christ was the Synagogue, because David had said. Psalm 95, V. 7: "*We are the people of his pasture, and the sheep of his hand*", and also because Abraham and David had been promised that the Messiah should be born of their race, because he was expected by the Hebrew people, foretold by the Prophets who were Hebrews, and that his advent, his acts, his passion, death and resurrection were prefigured in the sacrifices, worship and ceremonials of the Hebrew law.

97.

But, saving always the reverence due to the Holy Fathers and other Doctors, that explanation does not seem quite satisfactory. For it is an article of belief that the Church of the Faithful has been the only one in existence from the beginning of the world, and will thus endure to the end of time. The head of that Church is Jesus-Christ, the mediator between God and men, by whose contemplation all things were made and created. Indeed, the faith in the divine Trinity, though less explicitly, and the Incarnation of the Word were revealed to the first man, and by him taught his children, who, in their turn, taught them their descendants. And thus, although most men had strayed into idolatry and deserted the true faith, many kept the faith they had received from their fathers, and observing the law of nature, stayed in the true Church of the Faithful, as is noticed by Cardinal Tolet in reference to Job, who was a saint among idolatrous Gentiles. And, although God had conferred especial favours upon the Hebrew people, prescribed for them peculiar laws and ceremonials, and separated them from the Gentiles, yet those laws were not obligatory on the Gentiles, and the faithful Hebrews did not constitute a Church different from that of the Gentiles who professed their faith in one God and the coming of the Messiah.

98.

And thus it came to pass that even among the Gentiles there were some who prophesied the advent of Christ and the other dogmas of the Christian faith, to wit Balaam, Mercurius Trismegistus, Hydaspes, and the *Sibyls* mentioned by Lactantius, book i, ch. 6, as written by Baronius, *Apparat. Annal.*, No 18. That the Messiah was expected by the Gentiles is shown by many passages of Isaiah, and plainly testified by the prophecy of Jacob, the Patriarch, thus worded, Genesis, ch. 49, V. 10: *"The scepter shall not depart from Judah, nor a law-giver from between his feet, until Shiloh (he who is to be sent) come, and unto him shall the gathering of the people be."* — Likewise in the prophecy of Haggai, ch. 2, v. 8: *"I will shake all Nations, and the desire of all Nations shall come"*, which passage is thus commented by Cornelius a Lapide: *"The Gentiles before the advent of Christ, who believed in God and observed the law of nature, expected and desired Christ equally with the Jews.*"Christ himself disclosed and manifested himself to the Gentiles as well as to the Jews; for, at the same time as the Angel apprized the shepherds of his nativity, by means of the miraculous star he called the Magi to worship him, who, being Gentiles, were the first among the Nations, as the shepherds among the Jews, to acknowledge and worship Christ (*Vide* St Fulgentius, *Sermon 6, upon Epiphany*). In like manner, the advent of Christ was made known by preaching (I am not speaking of the Apostles) to the Gentiles before it was to the Jews. As is written by the Venerable Mother, Sister Maria of Agreda, in her *Life of Jesus Christ and the Blessed Virgin Mary*: "*When the Blessed Virgin Mary, fleeing with St Joseph, from the persecution of Herod, carried the Infant Jesus into Egypt, she tarried there seven years; and, during that time, the Blessed Virgin herself preached to the Egyptians thefaith of the true God and the advent of the Son of God in human flesh.*" Besides, the nativity of Christ was attended by numerous prodigies, not only in Judea, but also in Egypt, where the idols tumbled and the oracles were hushed; in Rome, where a spring of oil gushed out, a gold-coloured globe was seen to descend from the skies on earth, three suns appeared, and an extraordinary ring, variegated like a rainbow, encircled the disc of the sun; in Greece, where the oracle of Delphi was struck dumb, and Apollo, asked the reason of his silence by Augustus, who was offering up a sacrifice in his own palace where he had raised an altar to him, answered: "*A Hebrew child, who sways the Gods, and himself a God,*

Bids me quit my seat and return to the infernal regions;
Depart therefore from our altars, henceforward mute."

There were many more prodigies warning the Gentiles of the
advent of the Son of God: they have been collected from various
Authors, by Baronius, and are to be found in his *Apparat Annul.
Eccles.*, and Cornelius, *Commentary upon Haggai.*

99.

From all this it is clear that the Gentiles also belonged, like the
Jews, to the fold of Christ, that is, to the same Church of the
Faithful; it cannot therefore be correctly said that the words
of Christ: *"Other sheep I have, which are not of this fold"*, are
applicable to the Gentiles, who had, in common with the Hebrews,
the faith in God, the hope, prophecy, expectation, prodigies and
preaching of the Messiah.

100.

I therefore say that by the words *other sheep* may very well be
understood those rational Creatures or animals of whom we have
been treating hitherto. They being, as we have said, capable of
beatitude and damnation, and Jesus-Christ being the mediator
between God and man, as also every rational Creature (for rational
creatures attain to beatitude in consideration of the merits of
Christ, through the grace he confers upon them, without which
beatitude is impossible of attainment), every rational creature must
have cherished, at the same time as the faith in one God, the hope

of the advent of Christ, and have had the revelation of his nativity in the flesh and of the principles of the law of grace. Those were therefore the sheep which were not *of that human fold*, and which Christ had to bring; the sheep which were to hear His voice, that is, the announcement of His advent and of the evangelical doctrine, either directly through Himself, or through the Apostles; the sheep which, partaking with men of heavenly beatitude, were to realize *one fold and one shepherd.*

101.

To this interpretation, which I hold to be in no way improper, force is added by what we related, according to St Hieronymus, of that little man who requested St Anthony to *pray*, for him and his fellows, unto the common God, whom he knew to have suffered in human flesh. For, it implies that they were aware of the advent and of the death of Christ, whom, as God, they were anxious to propitiate, since they sought, to that effect, the intercession of St Anthony.

102.

Thereto tends also the fact mentioned by Cardinal Baronius (*Appar. Annal.* No 129), after Eusebius and Plutarch, as being one of the prodigies which took place at the time of the death of Christ. He relates that in the reign of the Emperor Tiberius, when Christ suffered, whilst mariners bound from Greece to Italy, were by night, and during a calm, in the vicinity of the Echinade Isles, their ship was brought close to land. All the crew heard a loud voice calling Tramnus, the master of the ship. He having answered to his name, the voice replied: *"When near such a marsh, announce that the great Pan is dead."* Which Tramnus having done, there arose suddenly, as from a numberless multitude, groans and shrieks. Doubtless, they were Demons, or corporeal Angels, or rational animals living near the marsh on account of their aqueous nature, and who, hearing of the death of Christ, described by the name of Great Pan, burst into tears and bewailing, like some of the Jews who, after witnessing the death of Christ, went home smiting their breasts (*Luke*, ch. 23, v. 48). From all that has been deduced above, it is therefore clear that there are such Demons, Succubi and Incubi, endowed with senses and subject to the passions thereof, as has been shown; who are born through generation and die through corruption, are capable of beatitude and damnation, more noble than man, by reason of the greater subtlety of their bodies, and who, when having intercourse with man, male or female, fall into the same sin as man when copulating with a beast, which is inferior to him. Also, it not infrequently occurs that those Demons slay the men, women or mares with whom they have had protracted intercourse; and the reason is that, being liable to sin whilst on the way to salvation, *in via*, they must likewise be open to repentance; and, in the same manner as a man, who habitually sins with a beast, is enjoined by his confessor to destroy that beast, with a view to suppressing the occasion of relapsing, it may likewise happen that the penitent demon should slay the animal with which it sinned, whether man or beast; nor will death thus occasioned to a man be reckoned a sin to the Demon, any more than death inflicted on a beast is imputed as a sin to man; for, considering the essential difference between a Demon of that kind and man, the man will be the same thing to the Demon as the beast is to man.

103.

I am aware that many, perhaps most of my readers, will say of me what the Epicureans 'and some Stoic Philosophers said of St Paul (*Acts of the Apostles*, ch. 17, V. 18). *"He seemeth to be a setter forth of strange gods"*, and will deride my doctrine. But they will none the less have to answer the foregoing arguments, to show what are those Incubi Demons, commonly called *Goblins*, who dread neither exorcisms, nor the holy things, nor the Cross of Christ, and to explain the various effects and phenomena related when propounding that doctrine.

104.

What we have hitherto deduced accordingly solves the question laid down Nos. 30 and 34, to wit: how a woman can be got with child by an Incubus Demon? In fact, it cannot be brought about by sperm assumed from a man, agreeably to the common opinion which we confuted, Nos. 31 and 32; it follows, therefore, that she is directly impregnated by the sperm of the Incubus, which, being an animal and capable of breeding, has sperm of its own. Arid thus is fully explained the begetting of Giants from the intercourse of the Sons of God with the Daughters of men: for that intercourse gave birth to Giants who, although like unto men, were of higher stature,

and, though begotten by Demons, and consequently of great
strength, yet equaled them neither in might nor in power. It is the
same with mules, which are intermediate, as it were, between the
kinds of animals from whose promiscuousness they are sprung,
and which excel indeed the most imperfect, but never equal the
most perfect: thus, the mule excels the ass, but does not attain the
perfection of the mare, which have begotten it.

105.

In confirmation of the above inference, we observe that animals
sprung from the mixing of different kinds do not breed, but are
barren, as is seen with mules. Now we do not read of Giants having
been begotten by other Giants, but of their having been born of the
Sons of God, that is Incubi, and the Daughters of men: being thus
begotten of the Demoniac sperm mixed with the human sperm, and
being, as it were, an intermediate species between the Demon and
man, they had no generative power.

106.

It may be objected that the sperm of Demons, which must, by
nature, be most fluid, could not mix with the human sperm, which
is thick, and that, consequently, no generation would ensue.

107.

I reply that, as has been said above, No 32, the generative power
lies in the spirit that comes from the generator at the same time
as the spumy and viscous ma.tter; it follows that, although most

liquid, the sperm of the Demon, being nevertheless material, can very well mix with the material spirit of the human sperm, and bring about generation.

108.

It will be retorted that, if the generation of Giants had really come from the combined sperms of Incubi and Women, Giants would still be born in our time, since there is no lack of women who have intercourse with Incubi, as is shown by the Acts of St Bernard and Peter of Alcantara, and other stories related by various authors.

109.

I reply that, as has been said above, No 81, from Guaccius, some of those Demons are earthly, some aqueous, some aerial, some igneous, and they all dwell in their respective element. Now, it is well known that animals are of larger size, according to the element they live in; thus with fishes, many of which are diminutive, it is true, as happens with animals that live on land; but, the element water being larger than the element earth, since the container is always larger than the contents, fishes as a species, surpass in size the animals that dwell on land, as shown by whales, tunnies, cachalots, and other cetaceous and viviparous fish which surpass by far all animals that live on land. Consequently, these Demons being animals, as has been shown, their size will be proportionate to the extent of the element they dwell in, according to their nature. And, air being more extensive than water, and fire than air, it follows that ethereal and Igneous Demons will by far surpass their earthly and aqueous fellows, both in stature and might. It would be to no purpose to instance, as an objection, birds which, although inhabitants of the air, a more extensive element than water, are smaller, as a species, than fishes and quadrupeds; for, if birds do indeed travel through the air by means of their wings, they no less belong to the element earth, where they rest; otherwise, some fishes that fly, such as the sea swallow, would have to be classed among aerial animals, which is not.

110.

Now, it must be observed that, after the flood, the air which surrounds our earthy and aqueous globe, became, from the damp of the waters, thicker than it had been before; and, damp being the principle of corruption, that may be the reason why men do not live as long as they did before the flood It is also on account of that thickness of the air that ethereal and igneous Demons, more corpulent than the others, can no longer dwell in that thick atmosphere, and if they do descend into it occasionally, do so only by force, much as divers descend into the depths of the sea.

111.

Before the flood, when the air was not yet so thick, Demons came upon earth and had intercourse with women, thus procreating Giants whose stature was nearly equal to that of the Demons, their fathers. But now it is not so: the Incubi Demons who approach women are aqueous and of small stature; that is why they appear in the shape of little men, and, being aqueous, they are most lecherous. Lust and damp go together: Poets have depicted Venus as born of the sea, in order to show, as explained by Mythologists, that lust takes its source in damp. When, therefore, Demons of short stature impregnate women nowadays, the children that are born are not giants, but men of ordinary size. It should, moreover, be known that when Demons have carnal intercourse with women in their own natural body, without having recourse to any disguise or artifice, the women do not see them, or if they do, see but an almost doubtful, barely sensible shadow, as was the case with the female we spoke of, No 28, who, when embraced by an Incubus, scarcely felt his touch. But, when they want to be seen by their mistresses, *atque ipsis delectationem in congressu carnali afferre*, they assume a visible disguise and a palpable body. By what means this is effected, is their secret, which our shortsighted Philosophy is unable to discover. The only thing we know is that such disguise or body could not consist merely in concrete air, since this must take place through condensation, and therefore by the influence of cold; a body thus formed would feel like ice, *et ita in coitu mulieres non delectaret*, but would give them pain; and it is the reverse that takes place.

112.

Being admitted the distinction between spiritual Demons, which have intercourse with witches, and Incubi, who have to do with women that are nowise witches, we have to weigh the grievousness of the crime in both cases.

113.

The intercourse of witches with Demons, from its accompanying circumstances, apostasy from the Faith, worshipping of the Devil, and so many other ungodly things related above, Nos. 12 to 24, is the greatest of all sins which can be committed by man; and, considering the enormity against Religion which is presupposed by coition with the Devil, *Demoniality* is assuredly the most heinous of all carnal crimes. But, taking the sin of the flesh as such, exclusive of the sins against Religion, *Demoniality* should be reduced to simple pollution. The reason is, and a most convincing one, that the Devil who has to do with witches is a pure spirit, has reached the goal and is damned, as has been said above; if, therefore, he copulates with witches, it is in a body assumed or made by himself, according to the common opinion of Theologians. Though set in motion, that body is not a living one; and it follows that the human being, male or female, *coiens cum tali corpore*, is guilty of the same offence as if copulating with an inanimate body or a corpse, which would be simple pollution, as we have shown elsewhere. It has, moreover, been truly observed by Cajetanus, that such intercourse can very well carry with it the disgraceful characteristics of other crimes, according to the body assumed by the Devil, and the part used: thus, if he should assume the body of a kinswoman or of a nun, such a crime would be incest or sacrilege; if coition took place in the shape of a beast, or in, *vase præpostero*, it would be Bestiality or Sodomy.

114.

As for intercourse with an Incubus, wherein is to be found no element, not even the least, of an offence against Religion, it is hard to discover a reason why it should be more grievous than Bestiality and Sodomy. For, as we have said above, if Bestiality is more grievous than Sodomy, it is because man degrades the dignity of his kind by mixing with a beast, of a kind much inferior to his own. But, when copulating with an Incubus, it is quite the reverse: for the Incubus, by reason of his rational and immortal spirit, is equal to man; and, by reason of his body, more noble because more subtle, he is more perfect and more dignified than man. Consequently, when having intercourse with an Incubus, man does not degrade, but rather dignifies his nature; and, taking that into consideration, *Demoniality* cannot be more grievous than Bestiality.

115.

It is, however, commonly held to be more grievous, and the reason I take to be this: that it is a sin against Religion to hold any communication with the Devil, either with or without compact, for instance by being habitually or familiarly connected with him, by asking his assistance, counsel or favor, or by seeking from him the revelation of things to be, the knowledge of things gone by, absent, or otherwise hidden. Thus, men and women, by mixing with Incubi, whom they do not know to be animals but believe to be devils, sin through intention, *ex conscientia erronea*, and their sin is intentionally the same, when having intercourse with Incubi, as if such intercourse took place with devils; in consequence, the grievousness of their crime is exactly the same.

FINIS

DÆMONIALITAS
The Latin Manuscript

1. Vocabulum Dæmonialitatis primo inventum reperio a Jo. Caramuele in sua Theologia fundamentali, *nec ante illum inveni Auctorem, qui de hoc crimine tanquam distincto a* Bestialitate locutus sit. Omnes enim Theologi Morales, secuti D. Thomam, 2.2., q. 154. in corp., *sub specie* Bestialitatis recensent omnem concubitum cum re non ejusdem speciei, *ut ibi loquitur D. Thomas, et proinde Cajetanus, in Commentario illius quæstionis et articuli, 2.2., q. 154., ad 3. dub., coitum cum Dæmone ponit in specie Bestialitatis; et Cajetanum sequitur Silvester, vᵒ Luxuria, Bonacina, de Matrim., q. 4., et alii.*

2. Sed revera D. Thomas in illo loco considerationem non habuit ad coitum cum Dæmone: ut enim infra probabimus, hic coitus non potest in specie specialissima Bestialitatis*comprehendi; et ut veritati cohæreat sententia S. Doctoris, dicendum est, quod in citato loco, quando ait, quod peccatum contra naturam,* alio modo si fiat per concubitum ad rem non ejusdem speciei vocatur Bestialitas: *sub nomine* rei non ejusdem speciei*intellexerit animal vivens, non ejusdem speciei cum homine: non enim usurpare potuit ibi nomen* rei pro re, puta, ente communi ad animatum et inanimatum: si enim quis coiret cum cadavere humano, concubitum haberet ad rem non ejusdem speciei cum homine (maxime apud Thomistas, qui formam corporeitatis humanæ negant in cadavere), quod etiam esset si cadaveri bestiali copularetur; et tamen talis coitus non esset bestialitas, sed mollities. Voluit igitur ibi D. Thomas præcise intelligere concubitum cum re vivente non ejusdem speciei cum homine, hoc est cum bruto, nullo autem modo comprehendere voluit coitum cum Dæmone.

3. Coitus igitur cum Dæmone, sive Incubo, sive Succubo (qui proprie est Dæmoni-
alitas), specie differt a Bestialitate, nec cum ea facit unam speciem specialissimam,
ut opinatus est Cajetanus: peccata enim contra naturam specie inter se distingui
contra opinionem nonnullorum Antiquorum, et Caramuelis, Summ. Armill.,
v. Luxur. n. 5., Jabien., eo. v. n. 6., Asten. lib. 2. tit. 46. art. 7., Caram. Theol. fun-
dam. post Filliucium, et Crespinum a Borgia, est opinio communis; et contraria
est damnata in proposit. 24. ex damnatis ab Alexandro VII.; tum quia singula
continent peculiarem, et distinctam turpitudinem repugnantem castitati, et
humanæ generationi; tum quia quodlibet ex iis privat bono aliquo secundum
naturam, et institutionem actus venerei, ordinati ad finem generationis humanæ;
tum quia quodlibet ipsorum habet diversum motivum, per se sufficiens ad
privandum *eodem bono diversimode, ut optime philosophatur Filliuc., tom. 2.*
c. 8. tract. 30. qu. 3. n° 142.; Cresp., q. mor. sel. contro.; Caramuel. q. 5. per tot.

4. Ex his autem infertur, quod etiam Dæmonialitas specie differt a Bestialitate:
singula enim ipsarum peculiarem, et distinctam turpitudinem castitati, ac hu-
manæ generationi repugnantem involvit; siquidem Bestialitas est copula cum bruto
vivente, ac sensibus et motu proprio prædito: Dæmonialitas autem est commixtio
cum cadavere (stando in sententia communi, quam infra examinabimus), nec sen-
sum, nec motum vitalem habente; et per accidens est, quod a Dæmone moveatur.
Quod si immunditia commissa cum brutali cadavere, vel humano, differt specie a
Sodomia et Bestialitate, ab ista differt pariter specie etiam Dæmonialitas, in qua,
juxta communem sententiam, homo cum cadavere concumbit accidentaliter moto.

5. Et confirmatur: quia in peccatis contra naturam, seminatio innaturalis (hoc
est, ea ad quam regulariter non potest sequi generatio) habet rationem generis;
subjectum vero talis seminationis est differentia constituens species sub tali genere,
unde si seminatio fiat in terram, aut corpus inanime, est mollities: si fiat cum ho-
mine in vase præpostero, est Sodomia; si fiat cum bruto, est bestialitas; quæ absque
controversia inter se specie differunt, eo quod terra, seu cadaver, homo, et brutum,
quæ sunt subjecta talis seminationis, specie differunt inter se. Sed Dæmon a bruto
non solum differt specie, sed plusquam specie: differunt enim per corporeum, et
incorporeum, quæ sunt differentiæ genericæ. Sequitur ergo quod seminationes
factæ cum aliis differunt inter se specie, quod est intentum.

6. Pariter, trita est doctrina Moralistarum fundata in Tridentino, sess. 14. c. 5. D.

Th. in 4. dist. 16. q. 3. art. 2., Vasquez, q. 91. art. 1. dub. 2. n. 6., Reginald. Valenz.
Medin. Zerola. Pesant. Sajir. Sott. Pitig. Henriquez apud Bonac. de Sac.disp. 5. q.
5. sect. 2. punct. 2. § 3. diffic. 3. n. 5., et tradita per Theologos, quod in confessione
manifestandæ sint tantum circumstantiæ quæ mutant speciem peccatorum. Si
igitur Dæmonialitas et Bestialitas sunt ejusdem speciei specialissimæ, sufficit in
confessione dicere: Bestialitatis peccatum commisi, *quantumvis confitens cum*
Dæmone concubuerit. Hoc autem falsum est: igitur non sunt ejusdem speciei
specialissimæ.

7. Quod si dicatur, aperiendum esse in confessione circumstantiam concubitus
cum Dæmone ratione peccati contra Religionem: peccatum contra Religionem
committitur, aut ex cultu, aut ex reverentia, aut ex deprecatione, aut ex pacto,
aut ex societate cum Dæmone (D. Thomas, 2. 2. q. 90. art. 2. et q. 95. art. 4. in
corp.); sed, ut infra dicemus, dantur Succubi, et Incubi, quibus nullum prædicto-
rum exhibetur, et tamen copula sequitur: igitur respectu istorum nulla intervenit
irreligiositas, et commixtio cum istis nullam habebit rationem ulteriorem, quam
*puri et simplicis coitus, qui, si est ejusdem speciei cum*Bestialitate, *sufficienter*
exprimetur dicendo: Bestialitatem commisi; *quod tamen falsum est.*

8. Ulterius in confesso est apud omnes Theologos Morales, quod longe gravior est
copula cum Dæmone, quam cum quolibet bruto; in eadem autem specie specialissi-
ma peccati non datur unum peccatum gravius altero, sed omnia æque gravia sunt;
perinde enim est coire cum cane, aut asina, aut equa; sequitur ergo, quod si Dæ-
monialitas est gravior Bestialitate, non sint ambo ejusdem speciei. Nec dicendum
gravitatem majorem in Dæmonialitate petendam esse ab irreligiositate, seu
superstitione ex societate cum Dæmone, ut scribit Cajetanus ad 2. 2. q. 154.,
ar. 11. § ad 3. in fine, quia hoc fallit in aliquibus Succubis et Incubis, ut supra
dictum est; tum quia gravitas major statuitur in Dæmonialitate præ Bestialitate,
in genere vitii contra naturam: major autem gravitas in illa supra istam ratione
irreligiositatis exorbitat ex illo genere, proinde non facit in illo genere, et ex se
graviorem.

9. Statuta igitur differentia specifica Dæmonialitatis a Bestialitate, ut gravitas
illius percipiatur in ordine ad pœnam de qua principaliter nobis tractandum est,
est necessarium inquirere quotupliciter Dæmonialitas accidat. Non desunt qui
sibi nimis scioli negant quod gravissimi Auctores scripsere, et quod quotidiana

constat experientia, Dæmonem scilicet tum Incubum, tum Succubum, non solum hominibus, sed etiam brutis carnaliter conjungi. Aiunt proinde esse hominum imaginationem, phantasmatibus a Dæmone perturbatis læsam, seu dæmoniaca esse præstigia: sicuti etiam Sagæ, seu Striges, sola imaginatione perturbata a Dæmone, sibi videntur assistere ludis, choreis, conviviis, et conventibus nocturnis, et carnaliter Dæmoni commisceri; nullo vero reali modo deferuntur corpore ad ejusmodi loca, et actiones, prout textualiter dicitur in quodam Capitulo, ac duobus Conciliis. Cap. Episcop. 26. q. 5., Conc. Ancyr. c. 24., Conc. Rom. 4. sub Damaso, *c. 5.* apud Laur. Epitom. v° Saga.

10. Sed non negatur, quin aliquando mulierculæ, illusæ a Dæmonibus, videantur nocturnis Sagarum ludis corporaliter interesse, dum tamen sola imaginaria visione ipsis hoc accidit: sicut etiam in somnis videtur nonnullis cum fœmina aliqua concumbere, et semen vere excernitur, non tamen concubitus ille realis est, sed tantum phantasticus, paratus non raro per illusionem diabolicam; et in hoc verissimum est quod habent citatum Capitulum et Concilia. Sed hoc non semper est; sed ut in pluribus, corpore deferuntur Sagæ ad ludos nocturnos, et vere carnaliter corpore conjunguntur Dæmoni, et Malefici non minus Dæmoni succubo miscentur, et hæc est sententia Theologorum, et jure consultorum Catholicorum, quos abunde citat Frater Franciscus Maria Guaccius in suo libro intitulato Compendium Maleficarum; *Grilland. Remig. Petr. Damian. Sylvest. Alphon. a Cast. Abul. Cajet. Senon. Crespet. Spine. Anan. apud Guaccium,* Comp. Malef., *c. 15. § Altera, quam verissimam... n. 69. lib. p.; quæ sententia confirmatur decem et octo exemplis, ibidem allatis et relatis per viros doctos et veridicos de quorum fide ambigendum non est, quibus probatur Maleficos et Sagas corporaliter ad ludos convenire, et cum Dæmonibus succubis et incubis corporaliter turpissime commisceri. Et pro omnibus sufficere debet auctoritas Divi Augustini, qui loquens de concubitu hominum cum Dæmonibus, sic ait lib. 15. de* Civitate Dei, *c. 23.:* «Et quoniam creberrima fama est, multique se expertos, vel ab eis qui experti essent, de quorum fide dubitandum non est, audivisse confirmant, Sylvanos et Faunos, quos vulgo Incubos vocant, improbos sæpe extitisse mulieribus, et earum appetiisse et peregisse concubitum. Et quosdam Dæmones, quos Dusios Galli nuncupant, hanc assidue immunditiam et tentare et efficere, plures talesque asseverant, ut hoc negare impudentia videatur.» *Hæc Augustinus.*

11. Prout autem apud diversos Auctores legitur, et pluribus experimentis compro-

batur, duplici modo Dæmon hominibus carnaliter copulatur: uno modo quo Maleficis et Sagis jungitur, alio modo quo aliis hominibus minime maleficis miscetur.

12. Quantum ad primum modum, non copulatur Dæmon Sagis, seu Maleficis, nisi præmissa solemni professione, qua iniquissimi homines Dæmoni addicuntur; quæ professio, ut ex variis Auctoribus referentibus confessiones Sagarum judiciales in tormentis factas, quas collegit Franciscus Maria Guaccius, Comp. Malef., c. 7., lib. 1., consistit in undecim ceremoniis.

13. Primo, ineunt pactum expressum cum Dæmone, aut alio Mago seu Malefico vicem Dæmonis gerente, et testibus præsentibus, de servitio diabolico suscipiendo: Dæmon vero viceversa honores, divitias, et carnales delectationes illis pollicetur. Guacc. loc. cit. fol. 34.

14. Secundo, abnegant catholicam fidem, subducunt se obedientiæ Dei, renuntiant Christo, et protectioni Beatissimæ Virginis Mariæ, ac Ecclesiæ omnibus sacramentis. Guacc. loc. cit.

15. Tertio, projiciunt a se Coronam, seu Rosarium B. V. M., Chordam S. P. Francisci, aut Corrigiam S. Augustini, aut Scapulare Carmelitarum, si quod habent, Crucem, Medaleas, Agnos Dei, et quidquid sacri aut benedicti gestabant, et pedibus ea proculcant. Guacc. loc. cit. fol. 35. Grilland.

16. Quarto, vovent in manibus Diaboli obedientiam, et subjectionem, eique præstant homagium et vassallagium, tangendo quoddam volumen nigerrimum. Spondent, quod nunquam redibunt ad fidem Christi, nec Dei præcepta servabunt, nec ulla bona opera facient, sed ad sola mandata Dæmonis attendent, et ad conventus nocturnos diligenter accedent. Guacc. loc. cit. fol. 36.

17. Quinto, spondent se enixe curaturos, et omni studio ac sedulitate procuraturos adducere alios mares et fœminas ad suam sectam, et cultum Dæmonis. Guacc. loc. cit.

18. Sexto, baptizantur a Diabolo sacrilego quodam baptismo, et abnegatis Patrinis et Matrinis baptismi Christi, et Confirmationis, et nomine, quod sibi fuit primo impositum, a Diabolo sibi assignantur Patrinus et Matrina novi, qui ipsos instru-

ant in arte maleficiorum, et imponitur nomen novum, quod plerumque scurrile est. Guacc. loc. cit.

19. Septimo, abscindunt partem propriorum indumentorum, et illam offerunt Diabolo in signum homagii, et Diabolus illam asportat, et servat. Guacc. loc. cit. *fol. 38.*

20. Octavo, format Diabolus circulum super terram, et in eo stantes Novitii Malefici et Sagæ firmant juramento omnia, quæ ut dictum est promiserunt. Guacc. loc. cit.

21. Nono, petunt a Diabolo deleri a libro Christi, et describi in libro suo, et profertur liber nigerrimus, quem tetigerunt præstando homagium, ut dictum est supra, et ungue Diaboli in eo exarantur. Guacc. loc. cit.

22. Decimo, promittunt Diabolo statis temporibus sacrificia, et oblationes; singulis quindecim diebus, vel singulo mense saltem necem alicujus infantis, aut mortale veneficium, et singulis hebdomadis alia mala in damnum humani generis, ut grandines, tempestates, incendia, mortem animalium, etc. Guacc. loc. cit. *fol. 40.*

23. Undecimo, sigillantur a Dæmone aliquo caractere, maxime ii, de quorum constantia dubitat. Caracter vero non est semper ejusdem formæ, aut figuræ: aliquando enim est simile lepori, aliquando pedi bufonis, aliquando araneæ, vel catello, vel gliri; imprimitur autem in locis corporeis magis occultis: viris quidem aliquando sub palpebris, aliquando sub axillis, aut labiis, aut humeris, aut sede ima, aut alibi; mulieribus autem plerumque in mammis, aut locis muliebribus. Porro sigillum, quo talia signa imprimuntur, est unguis Diaboli. Quibus peractis ad instructionem Magistrorum qui Novitios initiarunt, hi promittunt denuo, se nunquam Eucharistiam adoraturos; injuriosos Sanctis omnibus, et maxime B. V. M. futuros; conculcaturos ac conspurcaturos Sacras Imagines, Crucem, ac Sanctorum Reliquias; nunquam usuros Sacramentis, aut sacramentalibus, nisi ad maleficia; integram confessionem sacramentalem sacerdoti nunquam facturos, et suum cum Dæmone commercium semper celaturos. Et Diabolus vicissim pollicetur, se illis semper præsto futurum; se in hoc mundo votis eorum satisfacturum, et post mortem illos esse beaturum. Sic peracta professione solemni, assignatur singulis eorum Diabolus, qui appellatur Magistellus, *cum quo in partes secedunt, et carnaliter commiscentur: ille quidem in specie fœminæ, si initiatus est vir; in forma autem viri, et aliquando satyri, aliquando hirci, si fœmina est saga professa. Guacc. loc. cit. fol. 42 et 43.*

24. *Quod si quæratur ab Auctoribus, quomodo possit Dæmon, qui corpus non habet, corporalem commixtionem habere cum homine? Respondent communiter, quod Dæmon aut assumit alterius maris, aut fœminæ, juxta exigentiam, cadaver, aut ex mixtione aliarum materiarum effingit sibi corpus, quod movet, et mediante quo homini unitur. Et subdunt, quod quando fœminæ gaudent imprægnari a Dæmone (quod non fit, nisi in gratiam fœminarum hoc optantium), Dæmon se transformat in succubam, et juncta homini semen ab eo recipit; aut per illusionem nocturnam in somnis procurat ab homine pollutionem, et semen prolectum in suo nativo calore, et cum vitali spiritu conservat, et incubando fœminæ infert in ipsius matricem, ex quo sequitur conceptio. Ita multis citatis docet Guaccius, l. 1. c. 12., per totum, qui prædicta multis exemplis desumptis a variis Doctoribus confirmat.*

25. *Alio modo jungitur Dæmon tum Incubus, tum Succubus, hominibus, fœminis aut maribus, a quibus nec honorem, nec sacrificia, oblationes, maleficia, quæ a Sagis et Maleficis, ut supra dictum est, prætendit, recipit; sed ostendens deperdite amorem, nil aliud appetit, quam carnaliter commisceri cum iis quos amat. Multa sunt de hoc exempla, quæ ab Auctoribus referuntur, ut Menippi Lycii, qui fuit sollicitatus a quadam fœmina ad sibi nubendum, postquam cum ea multoties coivit; et detecta fœmina quænam esset a quodam Philosopho, qui convivio nuptiali intererat, et Menippo dixit illam esse* Compusam, *puta Dæmonem succubam, statim ejulans evanuit, ut narrat Cœlius Rodiginus,* Antiq. lib. 29, c. 5. Pariter adolescens quidam Scotus a Dæmone succuba omnium gratissima, quas vidisset, forma, quæ occlusis cubiculi foribus ad se ventitabat, blanditiis, osculis, amplexibus per multos menses fuit sollicitatus, ut secum coiret, ut scribit Hector Boethius, Hist. Scotor. lib. 8., quod tamen a casto juvene obtinere non potuit.

26. *Similiter, multas fœminas legimus ab Incubo Dæmone expetitas ad coitum, ipsisque repugnantibus facinus admittere, precibus, fletibus, blanditiis, non secus, ac perditissimus amasius procurasse animum ipsarum demulcere, et ad congressum inclinare; et quamvis aliquoties hoc eveniat ob maleficium, ut nempe Dæmon missus a maleficis hoc procuret: tamen non raro Dæmon ex se hoc agit, ut scribit Guaccius,* Comp. Mal., *lib. 3. c. 8., et non solum hoc evenit cum mulieribus, sed etiam cum equabus, cum quibus commiscetur; quæ si libenter coitum admittunt,*

ab eo curantur optime, ac ipsarum jubæ varie artificiosis et inextricabilibus nodis texuntur; si autem illum adversentur, eas male tractat, percutit, macras reddit, et tandem necat, ut quotidiana constat experientia.

27. Et quod mirum est, et pene incapabile, tales Incubi, qui Italice vocantur Folletti, *Hispanice* Duendes, *Gallice* Follets, *nec Exorcistis obediunt, nec exorcismos pavent, nec res sacras reverentur ad earum approximationem timorem ostendendo, sicuti faciunt Dæmones, qui obsessos vexant; quantumvis enim maligni Spiritus sint obstinati, nec parere velint Exorcistæ præcipienti, ut exeant a corporibus quæ obsident, tamen ad prolationem Sanctissimi Nominis Jesu, aut Mariæ, aut aliquorum Versuum Sacræ Scripturæ, impositionem Reliquiarum, maxime Ligni Sanctæ Crucis, approximationem Sacrarum Imaginum, ad os obsessi rugiunt, strident, frendent, concutiuntur, et timorem, ac horrorem ostendunt. Folletti vero nihil horum, ut dictum est, ostendunt, nec a divexatione, nisi post longum tempus, cessant. Hujus rei testis sum oculatus, et historiam recito quæ reipsa humanam fidem superat: sed testis mihi sit Deus quod puram veritatem multorum testimonio comprobatam describo.*

28. Viginti quinque abhinc annis plus, minusve, dum essem Lector Sacræ Theologiæ in Conventu Sanctæ Crucis Papiæ, reperiebatur in illa civitate honesta quædam fœmina maritata optimæ conscientiæ, et bonum habens ab omnibus eam agnoscentibus, maxime Religiosis, testimonium, quæ vocabatur Hieronyma; et habitabat in Parochia Sancti Michaelis. Hæc quadam die domi suæ panem pinserat, et per furnarium miserat ad illum decoquendum. Reportat panes coctos furnarius, et cum illis grandem quamdam placentam curiose elaboratam, conditam butyro, et pastulis Venetis, ut in ea civitate solent fieri placentæ hujusmodi. Renuit illa placentam recipere, dicens, se talem nullam fecisse. Replicat furnarius, se illa die alium panem coquendum non habuisse, nisi illum quem ab ea habuerat; oportere proinde, etiam placentam a se fuisse factam, licet minime de illa recordaretur. Acquievit fœmina, et placentam cum viro suo, filia quam habebat triennem, et famula comedit. Sequenti nocte, dum cubaret mulier cum viro suo, et ambo dormirent, expergefacta est a quadam tenuissima voce, velut acutissimi sibili ad ipsius aures susurrante, verbis tamen distinctis: interrogavit autem fœminam, num placenta illi placuisset? *Pavens fœmina cœpit se munire signo Crucis, et invocare sæpius nomina Jesu et Mariæ. Replicabat vox, ne paveret, se nolle illi nocere, immo quæcumque illi placerent paratum exequi, esse filo captum pulchritudinis suæ, et nil amplius desiderare, quam ejus amplexu frui. Tum fœmina sensit aliquem suaviantem ipsius genas, sed tactus ita levis, ac mollis, ac si esset gossipium subtilissime carminatum id, a quo tacta fuit. Respuit illa invitantem, nec ullum responsum illi dedit: sed jugiter nomen Jesu, et Mariæ repetebat, et se Crucis signo muniebat, et sic per spatium quasi horæ dimidiæ tentata fuit, et postea abscessit tentator.*

Sequenti mane fuit mulier ad Confessarium virum prudentem ac doctum, a quo fuit in fide confirmata et exhortata, ut viriliter, sicut fecerat, resisteret, et sacris Reliquiis se muniret. Sequentibus noctibus par priori fuit tentatio, et verbis, et osculis, et par etiam in muliere constantia. Hæc pertæsa talem ac tantam molestiam, ad Confessarii consultationem, et aliorum gravium virorum, per Exorcistas peritos fecit se exorcizare ad sciendum, num esset obsessa; et cum invenissent a nullo malo spiritu possideri, benedixerunt domui, cubiculo, lecto, et præceptum Incubo fecerunt, ne auderet molestiam amplius mulieri inferre. Sed omnia incassum; siquidem tentationem inceptam prosequebatur, ac si præ amore langueret, ploratus, et ejulatus emittebat ad mulierem demulcendam, quæ tamen gratia Dei adjuta semper viriliter restitit. Renovavit Incubus tentationem, ipsi apparens interdiu in forma pusionis, seu parvi homunculi pulcherrimi, cæsariem habens rutilam et crispam, barbamque fulvam ac splendentem velut aurum, glaucosque oculos, ut flos lini, incedebatque indutus habitu Hispanico. Apparebat autem illi quamvis cum ea alii morarentur; et questus, prout faciunt amantes, exercens, et jactando basia, solitasque preces repetendo tentabat mulierem, ut ad illius amplexus admitteretur. Videbatque, et audiebat illa sola præsentem ac loquentem, minime autem cæteri adstantes.

Perseverabat in illa constantia mulier, donec contra eam iratus Incubus, post aliquos menses blanditiarum novum persecutionis genus adortus est. Primo abstulit ab ea crucem argenteam plenam Reliquiis Sanctorum, et ceram benedictam, sive Agnum papalem B. Pontificis Pii V., quæ secum semper portabat; mox etiam annulos et alia jocalia aurea et argentea ipsius, intactis seris, sub quibus custodiebantur, in arca suffuratus est. Exinde cœpit illam acriter percutere, et apparebant post verbera contusiones, et livores in facie, brachiis, aliisque corporis partibus, quæ per diem unum, vel alterum perdurabant, mox in momento disparebant contra ordinem contusionis naturalis, quæ sensim paulatimque decrescit. Aliquoties ipsius infantulam lactentem cunis eripiebat, et illam, nunc super tecta in limine præcipitii locabat, nunc occultabat, nihil tamen mali in illa apparuit. Aliquoties totam domus supellectilem evertebat; aliquoties ollas, paropsides, et alia vasa testea minutatim frangebat, subinde fracta restituebat integra. Semel dum ipsa cum viro suo cubaret, apparens Incubus in forma solita, enixe deprecabatur ab ea concubitum, et dum ipsa de more constans resisteret, in furorem actus Incubus abscessit, et infra breve temporis spatium reversus est, secum ferens magnam copiam laminarum saxearum, quibus Genuenses in civitate sua et universa Liguria domos tegunt, et ex ipsis fabricavit murum circa lectum tantæ altitudinis, ut ejus conopeum adæquaret, unde necesse fuit scalis uti, si debuerunt de cubili surgere. Murus autem fuit absque calce, et ipso destructo, saxa in angulo seposita, quæ ibi per duos dies remanserunt visa a multis, qui ad spectaculum convenerant; et post biduum disparuerunt.

Invitaverat Maritus ejus in die S. Stephani quosdam amicos viros militares ad prandium, et pro hospitum dignitate dapes paraverat; dum de more lavantur manus ante accubitum, disparet in momento mensa parata in triclinio; disparent obsonia cuncta, olla, caldaria, patinæ, ac omnia vasa in coquina; disparent amphoræ, canthari, calices parati ad potum. Attoniti ad hoc stupent commensales, qui erant octo, inter quos Dux peditum Hispanus ad alios conversus ait: Ne paveatis, ista est illusio, sed pro certo mensa in loco in quo erat, adhuc est, et modo modo eam tactu percipiam. Hisque dictis circuibat cœnaculum manibus extentis tentans mensam deprehendere, sed cum post multos circuitus incassum laborasset, et nil præter ærem tangeret, irrisus fuit a cæteris; cumque jam grandis esset prandii hora, pallium proprium eorum unusquisque sumpsit propriam domum petiturus. Jam erant omnes prope januam domus in procinctu eundi associati a marito vexatæ mulieris, urbanitatis causa; cum grandem quendam strepitum in cœnaculo audiunt. Subsistunt parumper ad cognoscendum causam strepitus, et accurrens famula nuntiat in coquina vasa nova obsoniis plena apparuisse, mensamque in cœnaculo jam paratam esse restitutam. Revertuntur in cœnaculum, et stupent mensam mappis et manutergiis insolitis, salino, et lancibus insolitis argenteis, salsamentis, ac obsoniis, quæ domi parata non fuerant, instructam. A latere magna erecta erat credentia, supra quam optimo ordine stabant calices crystallini, argentini, et aurei cum variis amphoris, lagenis, cantharis plenis vinis exteris, puta Cretensi, Campano, Canariensi, Rhenano, etc. In coquina pariter in ollis, et vasis itidem in ea domo nunquam visis varia obsonia. Dubitarunt prius nonnulli ex iis eas dapes gustare, sed confirmati ab aliis accubuerunt, et exquisitissime omnia condita repererunt; ac immediate a prandio, dum omnes pro usu illius temporis ad ignem sedent, omnia ustensilia cum reliquiis ciborum disparuere, et repertæ sunt antiquæ domus supellectiles simul cum dapibus, quæ prius paratæ fuerant; et quod mirum est, convivæ omnes saturati sunt, ita ut nullus eorum cœnam sumpserit præ prandii lautitia. Quo convincitur cibos appositos reales fuisse, et non ex præstigio repræsentatos.

Interea effluxerant multi menses, ex quo cœperat hujusmodi persecutio: et mulier votum fecit B. Bernardino Feltrensi, cujus sacrum corpus veneratur in Ecclesia S. Jacobi prope murum illius urbis, incedendi per annum integrum indutam panno griseo, et chordulato, quo utuntur Fratres Minores, de quorum ordine fuit B. Bernardinus, ut per ipsius patrocinium a tanta incubi vexatione liberaretur. Et de facto die 28. Septembris, qui est pervigilium Dedicationis S. Michaelis Archangeli, et festum B. Bernardini, ipsa veste votiva induta est. Mane sequenti, quod est festum S. Michaelis, ibat vexata ad ecclesiam S. Michaelis, quæ ut diximus erat parochialis ipsius, circa medium mane, dum frequens populus ad illam confluebat; et cum pervenisset ad medium plateæ ecclesiæ, omnia ipsius indumenta et ornamenta ceciderunt in terram et rapta vento statim disparuerunt, ipsa relicta nuda. Adfuerunt sorte inter alios duo equites viri longævi, qui factum videntes dejectis ab humero propriis palliis mulieris nuditatem, ut potuerunt, velarunt, et rhedæ impositam ad propriam domum duxerunt. Vestes et jocalia quæ rapuerat Incubus, non restituit nisi post sex menses.

Multa alia, et quidem stupenda operatus est contra eam Incubus, quæ tædet excribere, et per multos annos in ea tentatione permansit, tandemque Incubus videns operam in ea perdere, destitit a tam importuna et insolita vexatione.

29. In hoc casu, et similibus qui passim audiuntur et leguntur, Incubus ad nullum actum contra Religionem tentat, sed solum contra castitatem. Hinc fit quod ipsi consentiens non peccat irreligiositate, sed incontinentia.

30. In confesso autem est apud Theologos et Philosophos, quod ex commixtione hominis, cum Dæmone aliquoties nascuntur homines et tali modo nasciturum esse Antichristum opinantur nonnulli Doctores: Bellarm., lib. 1. de Rom. Pont.cap. 12., Suarez, tom. 2. disp. 54. sec. 1.; Maluend., de Antichr. l. 2. c. 8. Immo observant, quod, qui gignuntur ab hujusmodi Incubis, naturali causa etiam evenit, ut nascantur grandes, robustissimi, ferocissimi, superbissimi, ac nequissimi ut scripsit Maluenda, loc. cit. § Ad illud; *et hujus rationem recitat ex Vallesio Archiat. Reggio. Sac. Philosoph. c. 8.*, dicente quod Incubi summittunt in uteros non qualecumque, neque quantumcumque semen, sed plurimum, crassissimum, calidissimum, spiritibus affluens et seri expers. Id vero est eis facile conquirere, deligendo homines calidos, robustos, et abundantes multo semine, quibus succumbant, deinde, et mulieres tales, quibus incumbant, atque utrisque voluptatem solito majorem afferendo, tanto enim abundantius emittitur semen, quanto cum majori voluptate excernitur. *Hæc Vallesius. Confirmat vero Maluenda supradicta, probando, ex variis et classicis Auctoribus, ex hujusmodi concubitu natos: Romulum ac Remum, Liv.* decad. 1.; *Plutarch.* in vit. Romul., et Parallel.; *Servium Tullium, sextum regem Romanorum, Dionys. Halicar. lib. 4., Plin. lib. 36. c. 27.; Platonem Philosophum, Laer. l. 9. de* Vit. Philos., *D. Hyeron. l. 1.* Controvers. Jovinian.; *Alexandrum Magnum, Plutarch.,* in vit. Alex. M.; *Quint. Curt., l. 4.* de Gest. Alex. M.; *Seleucum, regem Syriæ, Just.,* Hist. l. 15., *Appian.,* in Syriac.; *Scipionem Africanum Majorem, Liv.,* decad. 3. lib. 6.; Cæsarem Augustum Imperatorem, Sueton., in Octa.*c. 94.; Aristomenem Messenium, strenuissimum ducem Græcorum, Strabo,* de Sit. Orb. lib. 8., Pausan. de Rebus Græcor. lib. 3.; et Merlinum, seu Melchinum Anglicum ex Incubo et Filia Caroli Magni Moniali, Hauller, volum. 2. Generat. 7.; quod etiam de Martino Luthero, perditissimo Heresiarca, scribit Cocleus apud Maluendam, deAntich. lib. 2. c. 6. § Cæterum.

31. Salva tamen tot, et tantorum Doctorum, qui in ea opinione conveniunt, reverentia, non video, quomodo ipsorum sententia possit subsistere; tum quia, ut optime opinatur Pererius, tom. 2. in Genes. cap. 6. disp. 5., tota vis et efficacia humani seminis consistit in spiritibus, qui difflantur, et evanescunt, statim ac sunt extra genitalia vasa, a quibus foventur, et conservantur, ut scribunt Medici. Nequit proinde Dæmon semen acceptum conservare, ita ut aptum sit generationi, quia vas, quodcumque sit illud, in quo semen conservare tentaret, oporteret, quod caleret calore assimetro a nativo organorum humanæ generationis; similarem enim a nullo alio præterquam ab organis ipsis habere potest. In vase autem non calente vi tali calore, sed alieno, spiritus resolvuntur, nec sequi potest generatio. Tum quia generatio actus vitalis est, per quem homo generans de propria substantia semen defert per organa naturalia ad locum generationi congruentem. In casu autem delatio seminis non potest esse actus vitalis hominis generantis, quia ab eo non infertur in matricem; proinde nec dici potest, quod homo cujus est semen, generet fœtum, qui ex eo nascitur. Neque Incubus ipsius pater dici potest; quia de ipsius substantia semen non est. Hinc fiet, quod nascetur homo, cujus nemo pater sit, quod est incongruum. Tum quia in patre naturaliter generante duplex causalitas concurrit, nempe materialis, quia semen, quod materia generationis, ministrat, et efficiens, quia agens principale est in generatione, ut communiter statuunt Philosophi. In casu autem nostro homo ministrando solum semen, puram materiam exhiberet absque ulla actione in ordine ad generationem; proinde non posset dici pater filii, qui nasceretur: et hoc est contra id, quod homo genitus ab Incubo non est illius filius, sed est filius ejus viri, a quo Incubus semen sumpsit.

32. Præterea omni probabilitate caret quod scribit Vallesius, et ex eo recitavimus supra n° 30.; mirorque a doctissimi viri calamo talia excidisse. Notissimum enim est apud Physicos, quod magnitudo fœtus non est a quantitate molis, sed est a quantitate virtutis, hoc est spirituum in semine: ab ea enim tota generationis ratio dependet, ut optime testatur Michael Ettmullerus, Instit. Medic. Physiolog. car. 22. thes. 1. fol. m. 39., scribens: Tota generationis ratio dependet a spiritu genitali sub crassioris materiæ involucro excreto; ista materia seminis crassa nullo modo, vel in utero subsistente, vel ceu materia fœtum constituente: sed solus spiritus genitalis maris unitus cum spiritu genitali mulieris in poros uteri, seu quod rarius fit in tubos uteri se insinuat, indeque uterum fecundum reddit. *Quid ergo facere potest magna quantitas seminis ad fœtus magnitudinem? Præterea nec semper verum est, quod tales geniti ab Incubis magnitudine molis corporeæ insignes sint: Alexander enim Magnus, qui, ut diximus, natus taliter scribitur, statura pusillus erat; unde Carmen,*
Magnus Alexander corpore parvus erat.
Item quamvis taliter concepti supra cæteros homines excellant, non tamen hoc semper est in vitiis, sed aliquando in virtutibus etiam in moralibus, ut patet in Scipione Africano, Cæsare Augusto, et Platone Philosopho, de quibus Livius, Suetonius et Laertius respective scribunt, quod optimi in moribus fuere; ut proinde arguere possimus, quod si alii eodem modo geniti pessimi fuere, hoc non fuerit ex hoc, quod fuerint ab Incubo geniti, sed quia tales ex proprio arbitrio extitere. Pariter ex textu Sacræ Scripturæ, Gen. c. 6. v. 4., habemus quod gigantes nati sunt ex concubitu filiorum Dei cum filiabus hominum, et hoc ad litteram sacri textus. Gigantes autem homines erant statura magna, *ut eos vocat Baruch, c. 3. v. 26, et excedente communem hominum proceritatem. Monstruosa statura, robore, latrociniis, et tyrannide insignes; unde Gigantes per sua scelera fuerunt maxima, et potissima causa Diluvii, ait Cornelius a Lapid.* in Gen. c. 6. v. 4. § Burgensis. *Non quadrat autem quorumdam expositio, quod nomine filiorum Dei veniant filii Seth, et vocabulo filiarum hominum filiæ Cain, eo quod illi erant pietati, Religioni, et cæteris virtutibus addicti, descendentes autem a Cain viceversa: nam salva*

opinantium, Chrysost. Cyrill. Theodor. Rupert. Ab., et Hilar. in Psalm. 132. apud Cornel. a Lap. c. 6. G. v. 2. § Verum dies, *reverentia, talis expositio non cohæret sensui patenti litteræ; ait enim Scriptura, quod ex conjunctione talium nati sunt homines monstruosæ proceritatis corporeæ: ante illam ergo tales gigantes non extiterunt: quod si ex ea orti sunt, hoc non potuit esse ex eo, quod filii Seth coivissent cum filiabus Cain, quia illi erant staturæ ordinariæ, prout etiam filiæ Cain, unde oriri ex his naturaliter non potuerunt, nisi filii staturæ ordinariæ; si ergo monstruosa statura filii nati sunt ex tali conjunctione, hoc fuit, quia non fuerunt prognati ex ordinaria conjunctione viri cum muliere, sed ex Incubis dæmonibus qui ratione naturæ ipsorum optime possunt vocari filii Dei, et in hac sententia sunt Philosophi Platonici, et Franciscus Georgius Venetus, tom. 1. problem. 74.: nec dissentiunt ab eadem Joseph. Hebræus, Philo Judæus, S. Justinus Martyr, Clemens Alexandrinus, et Tertullianus. Joseph. Hebræus,* Antiq. l. 1., Philo, l. de Gigant., S. Justinus M., Apolog. 1., Clemens Alex., lib. 3., Tertull., lib. de Habit. Mul., *apud Cornel., loc. cit., Hugo de S. Victor.,* Annot. in Gen., c. 6., *qui opinantur illos fuisse Angelos quosdam corporeos qui in luxuriam cum mulieribus delapsi sunt, ut enim infra ostendemus istæ duæ sententiæ in unam, et eamdem conveniunt.*

33. *Si ergo Incubi tales, ut fert communis sententia, Gigantes genuerunt, accepto semine ab homine, juxta id, quod supra dictum est, non potuerunt ex illo semine nasci nisi homines ejusdem staturæ plus, minusve, cum eo a quo semen acceptum est: nec enim facit ad altiorem corporis staturam major seminis quantitas, ita ut attracta insolite a Dæmone, dum succubus fit homini, augeat ultra illius staturam enormiter corpus ab eo geniti; quia, ut supra diximus, hoc residet in spiritu, et non in mole seminis: ut proinde necesse sit concludere, quod ab alio semine, quam humano hujusmodi gigantes nati sint, et proinde Dæmon Incubus non humano, sed alio semine utatur ad generationem. Quid igitur dicendum?*

34. *Quantum ad hoc, sub correctione Sanctæ Matris Ecclesiæ, et mere opinative dico, Incubum Dæmonem dum mulieribus commiscetur, ex proprio ipsius semine hominem generare.*

35. *Paradoxa in fide, et parum sana nonnullis videbitur hæc opinio; sed lectorem meum deprecor, ut judicium non præcipitet de ea: ut enim incivile est nondum tota lege perspecta judicare, ut Celsus, lib. 24. ff. de legib. et S. C., ait, ita neque damnanda est opinio, nisi prius examinatis, ac solutis argumentis, quibus inniti-*

tur. Ad probandam igitur supradatam conclusionem, nonnulla sunt necessario præmittenda.

36. Præmittendum primo de fide est, quod dentur Creaturæ pure spirituales nullo modo de materia corporea participantes, prout habetur ex Concillio Lateranensi, sub Innocentio Tertio, c. Firm. de Sum. Trin. et Fid. Cath. Conc. Eph. in Epist. Cyrill. ad Reggia, et alibi. Hujusmodi autem sunt Angeli beati, et Dæmones damnati ad ignem perpetuum. Quamvis vero nonnulli Doctores, Bann. par. 1. q. 5. ar. 1. Can. de Loc. Theol. l. 5. c. 5. Sixt. seu Bibliot. San. l. 5. annot. 8., Mirand. Sum. Concil. v°.Angelus, *Molina, p. 1. q. 50., a. 1., Carranz., Annot. ad Synod.7., etiam post Concilium illud docuerint spiritualitatem Angelorum et Dæmonum non esse de fide, ita ut nonnulli alii, Bonav. in lib. 2. sent. dist. 3. q. 1., Scot. de* Anim. q. 15., Cajet. in Gen. c. 4., Franc. Georg. Problem. l. 2. c. 57., August. Hyph., de Dæmon., *l. 3. c. 3., scripserint illos esse corporeos, et proinde Angelos Dæmonesque corpore et spiritu constare non esse propositionem hæreticam, neque erroneam probet Bonaventura Baro, Scot. Defens. tom. 9. apolog. 2., act. 1., p. §* 7.: tamen quia Concilium ipsum statuit de fide tenendum, Deum esse Creatorem omnium visibilium, et invisibilium, spiritualium, et corporalium, qui utramque de nihilo condidit creaturam spiritualem et corporalem Angelicam, videlicet ut mundanam: *ideo dico de fide esse quasdam creaturas dari mere spirituales, et tales esse Angelos, non quidem omnes, sed quosdam.*

37. Inaudita forsan erit sententia hæc, sed non destituta erit probabilitate. Si enim a Theologis tanta inter Angelos diversitas specifica, et proinde essentialis statuitur, ut in via D. Thomæ, p. p., q. 50., ar. 4., plures Angeli nequeant esse in eadem specie, sed quilibet Angelus propriam speciem constituat, profecto nulla invenitur repugnantia, quod Angelorum nonnulli sint purissimi spiritus, et proinde excellentissimæ naturæ, alii autem corporei, et minus excellentes, et eorum differentia petatur per corporeum, et incorporeum. Accedit quod hac sententia facile solvitur alias insolubilis contradictio inter duo Concilia Œcumenica, nempe Septimam Synodum generalem, et dictum Concilium Lateranense: siquidem in illa Synodo, quæ est secunda Nicæna, actione quinta, productus est liber Joannis Thessalonicensis scriptus contra quemdam Philosophum gentilem, in quo ita habetur: De Angelis, et Archangelis, atque eorum Potestatibus, quibus nostras Animas adjungo, ipsa Catholica Ecclesia sic sentit, esse quidem intelligibiles, sed non omnino corporis expertes, et insensibiles, ut vos Gentiles dicitis, verum tenui corpore præditos, et æreo, sive igneo, sicut scriptum est: qui facit Angelos suos spiritus, et ministros suos ignem urentem. *Et infra:* Quamquam autem non sint ut nos, corporei, utpote ex quatuor elementis, nemo tamen vel Angelos, vel Dæmones, vel Animas dixerit incorporeas: multoties enim in proprio corpore visi sunt ab illis, quibus Dominus oculos aperuit. *Et cum omnia lecta fuissent coram Patribus synodaliter congregatis, Tharasius, Patriarcha Constantinopolitanus, poposcit adprobationem Sanctæ Synodi his verbis:* Ostendit Pater, quod Angelos pingi oporteat, quoniam circumscribi possunt, et ut homines apparuerunt. *Synodus autem uno ore respondit:* Etiam, Domine.

38. Hanc autem Conciliarem adprobationem de materia ad longum pertractata a D. Joanne in libro coram Patribus lecto, statuere articulum fidei circa corporeitatem Angelorum, perspicuum est: unde ad tollendam contradictionem hujus, cum allata definitione Concilii Lateranensis multum desudant Theologi. Unus enim, Suarez, de Angelis, *ait, quod Patres non contradixerunt tali asserto de corporeitate Angelorum, quia non de illa re agebatur. Alius, Bann., in p. p. q. 10., ait, quod Synodus adprobavit conclusionem, nempe Angelos pingi posse, non tamen adprobavit rationem,* quia corporei sunt. *Alius, Molin., in p. p., q. 50. a. 1., ait, quod definitiones Conciliares in illa Synodo factæ sunt solum* actione septima, *proinde ea quæ habentur in actionibus præcedentibus non esse definitiones de fide. Alii, Joverc. et Mirand., Sum. Conc., scribunt nec Nicænum, nec Lateranense Concilium intendisse definere de fide quæstionem; et Nicænum quidem locutum fuisse juxta opinionem Platonicorum, quæ ponit Angelos corporeos, et tunc prævalebat; Lateranense autem locutum esse juxta mentem Aristotelis, qui, l. 12.*Metaphys., *tex. 49., ponit intelligentias incorporeas, quæ sententia contra Platonicos apud plerosque Doctores invaluit expost.*

39. Sed quam frigidæ sint istæ responsiones nemo non videt, ac eas minime satisfacere oppositioni palmariter demonstrat Bonaventura Baro, Scot. Defens., tom. 9., apolog. 2., actio. 1., § 2. per totum. *Proinde ad tollendam contradictionem Conciliorum dicendum est, Nicænum locutum esse de una, Lateranense autem de alia specie Angelorum, et illam quidem corpoream, hanc vero penitus incorpoream; et sic conciliantur, aliter irreconciliabilia Concilia.*

40. Præmittendum 2°., nomen Angeli esse nomen officii, non naturæ, ut concorditer scribunt S. S. Patres: Ambros. in c. 1. epist. ad Hebr., *Hilarius, l. 5.* de Trin.,

Augustinus, lib. 15. de Civit. Dei. c. 23., Gregorius, Hom. 34. in Evang., Isidorus, l. de Sum. Bonit., c. 12.; unde præclare ait D. Ambrosius: Angelus non ex eo quod est spiritus, ex eo quod agit, Angelus, quia Angelus Græce, Latine Nuntius dicitur; sequitur igitur ex hoc, quod illi, qui ad aliquod ministerium a Deo mittuntur, sive spiritus sint, sive homines, Angeli vocari possunt; et de facto ita vocantur in Scripturis Sacris: nam de Sacerdotibus, Concionatoribus, ac Doctoribus, qui tanquam Nuntii Dei explicant hominibus divinam voluntatem, dicitur, Malach. c. 2. v. 7.: Labia Sacerdotis custodient scientiam, et legem requirent ex ore ejus, quia Angelus Domini exercituum est. *D. Joannes Baptista ab eodem Propheta, c. 3. v. 1., vocatur Angelus, dum ait:* Ecce ego mitto Angelum meum, et præparabit viam ante faciem meam. *Et hanc prophetiam esse ad litteram de S. Joanne Baptista testatur Christus Dominus in* Evangelio Matthæi, *11., v. 10. Immo et ipse Deus, quia fuit missus a Patre in mundum ad evangelizandum legem gratiæ, vocatur Angelus. Ita in prophetia Isaiæ, c. 9. v. 6., juxta versionem Septuaginta:* Vocabitur nomen ejus magni consilii Angelus, *et clarius in Malachiæ c. 3. v. 1.,:* Veniet ad templum sanctum suum Dominator quem vos quæritis, et Angelus testamenti, quem vos vultis. *Quæ prophetia ad litteram est de Christo Domino. Sequitur igitur nullum absurdum sequi ex hoc, quod dicimus Angelos quosdam esse corporeos, nam et homines, qui corpore constant, Angeli vocabulo efferuntur.*

41. Præmittendum 3°., nondum rerum naturalium, quæ sunt in Mundo, satis perspectam esse existentiam, aut naturam, ut proinde aliquid negandum sit ex eo, quod de illo nunquam alias dictum, aut scriptum fuerit. Patet enim tractu temporis detectas esse novas terras, quas Antiqui nostri ignorarunt, novaque animalia, herbas, plantas, fructus, semina nunquam alias visa; et si pervia esset Terra Australis incognita, cujus indagatio, et lustratio a multis hucusque incassum tentata est, adhuc nova nobis alia panderentur. Patet adhuc, quod per inventionem Microscopii, et alias machinas, et organa Philosophiæ experimentales modernæ, sicut etiam per exactiorem indaginem Anatomistarum, multarum rerum naturalium existentiam, vires, naturamque tum innotuisse, tum dietim innotescere, quæ præcedentes Philosophi ignorarunt, ut patet in auro fulminante, phosphoro, et centum aliis chymicis experimentis, circulatione sanguinis, venis lacteis, vasis lymphaticis, et aliis hujusmodi quæ nuper Anatomistæ adinvenerunt. Proinde ineptum erit aliquod exsibillare ex hoc quod de eo nullus Antiquorum scripserit, attento maxime Logicorum axiomate, quod locus ab auctoritate negativa non tenet.

42. *Præmittendum 4°., quod in Sacra Scriptura, et Ecclesiasticis traditionibus non traditur nisi id, quod ad Animæ salutem necessarium est, quoad credendum, sperandum et amandum; unde inferre non licet ex eo, quod nec ex Scriptura, nec ex traditione aliquod habetur, proinde negandum sit, quod illud tale existat: aut nos quidem Fides docet, Deum per Verbum suum omnia creasse visibilia, et invisibilia; pariterque ex Jesu Christi Domini nostri meritis tum gratiam, tum gloriam omni, et cuivis rationali creaturæ conferri. Num autem alius Mundus a nostro, quem incolimus, sit; et in eo alii homines non ab Adam prognati, sed alio modo a Deo creati existant (sicut ponunt illi, qui lunarem globum habitatum opinantur); pariterque num in hoc Mundo, quem incolimus, aliæ existant creaturæ rationales ultra homines, et Spiritus Angelicos, quæ regulariter hominibus sint invisibiles, et per accidens, et earum executiva potentia fiant visibiles: hoc nullo modo spectat ad fidem, et hoc scire, aut ignorare non est ad salutem hominis necessarium, sicut nec scire rerum omnium physicarum numerum aut naturam.*

43. *Præmittendum 5°., nullam inveniri repugnantiam, nec in Philosophia, nec in Theologia, quod dari possint creaturæ rationales constantes spiritu et corpore, aliæ ab homine, quia si esset repugnantia hoc esset vel ex parte Dei (et hoc non quia ipse omnipotens est), vel ex parte rei creabilis; et neque hoc, quia sicut creatura mere spiritualis, ut Angeli, creata est, et mere materialis, ut Mundus, et partim spiritualis, partim corporea, corporeitate terrestri, et crassa, ut homo, ita creabilis est creatura constans spiritu rationali, et corporeitate minus crassa, sed subtiliore, quam sit homo. Et profecto post Resurrectionem Anima Beatorum erit unita corpori glorioso dote subtilitatis donato: ut proinde concludi posset, potuisse Deum creare creaturam rationalem corpoream, cui naturaliter indita sit corporis subtilitas, sicut per gratiam corpori glorioso confertur.*

44. *Astruitur autem magis talium creaturarum possibilitas ex solutione argumentorum, quæ contra positam conclusionem fieri possunt, pariterque ex responsione ad interrogationes, quæ possunt circa eam formari.*

45. *Prima interrogatio est, an tales creaturæ dicendæ essent animalia rationalia? Quod si sic, quomodo different ab homine, cum quo communem haberent definitionem?*

46. *Respondeo quod essent animalia rationalia sensibus, et organis corporis*

prædita, sicut homo: differrent autem ab homine non solum ratione corporis tenuioris, sed etiam materiæ. Homo siquidem ex crassiore elementorum omnium parte, puta ex luto, nempe aqua et terra crassa formatus est, ut constat ex Scriptura, Gen. 2. v. 7.; ista vero formata essent ex subtiliore parte omnium, aut unius, seu alterius elementorum; ut proinde alia essent terrea, alia aquea, alia ærea, et alia ignea, et ut eorum definitio cum hominis definitione non conveniret, addendum esset definitioni hominis crassa materialitas sui corporis, per quam a dictis animalibus differret.

47. *Secunda interrogatio est, quandonam hujus modi animalia fuissent condita, et num cum brutis producta a terra, aut ab aqua, ut quadrupedia, et aves respective; an vero a Domino Deo formata, ut fuit homo?*

48. *Respondeo quod de fide est, quod posito, quod existant de facto, creata sint a principio Mundi: sic enim definitur a Concilia Lateranensi (Firm. de Sum. Trinit. et Fide cathol.); nempe quod Deus sua omnipotenti virtute simul ab initio temporis utramque de nihilo condidit creaturam, spiritualem et corporalem. Sub illa etenim Creaturarum generalitate etiam illa animalia essent comprehensa. Quo vero ad eorum formationem, decuisse ipsorum corpus a Deo ministerio Angelorum formatum fuisse, sicut a Deo formatum legimus corpus hominis, quia ipsi copulandus erat spiritus immortalis, quandoquidem spiritus incorporeus, et proinde nobilissimus corpori pariter originaliter nobiliori cæteris brutis jungendus erat.*

49. *Tertia interrogatio, an talia animalia habuissent originem ab uno solo, velut omnes homines ab Adam, an vero plura simul formata essent sicut fuit de cæteris animantibus a terra, et aqua productis, in quibus fuerunt Mares, et Fœminæ quæ speciem per generationem conservant? Et si hoc oporteret inter talia animalia esse distinctionem sexus; ipsa nasci, et interire; passionibus sensus affici, nutriri, crescere; et tunc quo alimenta vescerentur, esset quærendum; præterea an vitam socialem ducerent, ut homines; qua politica regerentur; num urbes ad habitandum struxissent; num artes, studia, possessiones, et bella inter ea essent, sicut est in hominibus.*

50. *Respondeo: potuit esse quod omnia ab uno, velut homines ab Adam, sint progenita; potuit pariter esse, quod ex iis multi mares, et plures fœminæ fuissent formatæ, a quibus per generationem eorum species essent propagatæ. Ultro ad-*

mitteremus talia animalia oriri, et mori; mares alios, alias fœminas inter ea esse; passionibus, sensibus agitari velut homines; nutriri et crescere secundum molem sui corporis; cibum autem ipsorum non crassum qualem requirit crassities corporis humani, sed substantiam tenuem, et vaporosam emanantem per effluvia spirituosa a rebus physicis pollentibus corpusculis maxime volatilibus, ut nidor carnium maxime assatarum, vapor vini, fructuum, florum, aromatum, a quibus copiosa hujusmodi effluvia usque ad totalem partium subtiliorum, ac volatilium evaporationem scaturiunt. Talia autem animalia civilem vitam ducere posse, et inter ea distinctos esse gradus dominantium ac servientium pro conditione naturæ ipsorum, artesque, scientias, ministeria, exercitia, loca, mansiones, ac alia necessaria ad eorum conservationem, nullam penitus importat repugnantiam.

51. Quarta interrogatio est, qualis esset eorum corporis figuratio, an humanam, an aliam formam, et qualem haberent, et an partes corporis ipsorum haberent ordinem essentialem inter se, ut corpora cæterorum animalium, an vero accidentalem tantum, ut corpora fluidarum substantiarum, ut olei, aquæ, nubis, fumi, etc.; et num substantiæ suarum partium organicarum diversimode constarent, ut organa hominum, in quibus sunt aliæ partes crassissimæ, ut ossa, aliæ minus crassæ, ut cartilagines, aliæ tenues, ut membranæ.

52. Respondeo, quod quantum ad figuram corpoream nihil certi affirmare debemus, aut possumus, cum talis figura non sit exacte nobis sensibilis, nec quoad visum, nec quoad tactum præ sui corporis tenuitate, ac perspicacitate; qualis proinde vere sit, noverent ipsi, aliique, qui substantias immateriales intuitive cognoscere possunt. Quoad congruentiam et probabilitatem dico, illa referre speciem corporis humani, cum aliquo distinctivo a corpore humano, nisi forte ad hoc sufficiat sua ipsorum tenuitas. Ducor, quia corpus humanum plasmatum a Deo perfectissimum est, inter animalia quæque, et cum cætera bruta in terram sint prona, eo quia anima eorum mortalis est, Deus, ut ait poeta Ovid., Metamorphos.
Os homini sublime dedit, cœlumque tueri
Jussit, et erectos ad sidera tollere vultus;
quia anima hominis immortalis ordinata est ad cœlestem mansionem. Cum igitur animalia, de quibus loquimur, spiritum haberent immaterialem, rationalem, ac immortalem, et proinde capacem beatitudinis, ac damnationis, congruum est, quod corpus, cui talis spiritus copulatur, simile sit omnium animalium nobilissimo, corpori humano. Ex hac positione sequitur, quod ejus corporis partes ordinem inter

se essentialem habere deberent; nec enim pes capiti, aut ventri manus conjungi deberet: sed congrua membrorum essentiali dispositione ordinata, ut essent idonea ministeriis propriis perficiendis. Quo autem ad partes componentes ipsarum organa, dico quod necessarium esset, ut nonnullæ ipsarum essent solidiores, aliæ minus solidæ, aliæ tenues, aliæ tenuissimæ pro necessitate operationis organicæ. Nec contra hanc positionem facile potest asseri tenuitas ipsorum corporum: quippe soliditas aut crassities organicarum partium, de qua dicimus, non esset talis simpliciter, sed comparative ad alias partes tenuiores. Et hoc patere potest in omnibus corporibus fluidis naturalibus, ut vino, oleo, lacte, etc.; quantumvis enim omnes partes in ipsis videantur homogeneæ, ac similares, non tamen ita est; nam in ipsis est pars terrea, pars aquea, sal fixum, sal volatile, et pars sulfurea, quæ omnia manipulatione spargirica oculis subjici possunt. Ita esset in casu nostro: posito enim quod talium animalium corpora subtilia, et tenuia, ut corpora naturalia fluida, velut aqua, et ær, essent, non tamen tolleretur, quin in ipsorum partibus diversæ inter se essent qualitates, et aliquæ ipsarum comparative ad alias essent solidæ, et aliæ tenuiores, quamvis totum corpus ex ipsis compositum tenue dici posset.

53. Quod si dicatur, quod hæc repugnant positioni supra firmatæ, circa partium essentialem ordinationem inter se: quandoquidem videmus, quod in corporibus fluidis, ac tenuibus una pars non servat ordinem essentialem ad aliam, sed accidentalem tantum, ita ut hæc pars vini, quæ modo alteri parti contigua est, mox inverso vase, aut moto vino, alteri parti unitur, et sic omnes partes diversam positionem habent quantumvis semper idem vinum sit, et ex hoc sequeretur, quod talium animalium corpora figurata stabiliter non essent, et consequenter, nec organica.

54. Respondeo negando assumptum; etenim in corporibus fluidis, quamvis non appareat, manet tamen essentialis partium ordinatio, qua stante stat in suo esse compositum, et hoc patet manifeste in vino: expressum enim ab uvis videtur liquor totaliter homogeneus, non tamen ita est; in eo enim sunt partes crassæ, quæ tractu temporis subsident in doliis: sunt etiam partes tenues, quæ evaporant: sunt partes fixæ, ut tartarus, sunt partes volatiles, ut sulphur, sive spiritus ardens; sunt partes mediæ inter volatile ac fixum, ut phlegma. Partes istæ ordinem essentialem inter se mutant; nam statim, ac expressum est ab uvis, et mustum dicitur sulphur, sive spiritus volatilis, ita implicatum manet particulis tartari, qui fixus est, ut nullo modo avolare valeat.

55. Hinc est, quod a musto recenter ab uvis expresso nullo modo potest distillari spiritus sulphureus, qui communiter vocatur aqua vitæ: *sed post quadraginta dies fermentationis particulæ vini ordinem mutant, ita ut spiritus, qui alligati erant particulis tartareis, et propria volatilitate eas suspensas tenebant, et vicissim ab eis, ne possent avolare detinebantur, ac tartareis particulis separantur, et divulsi, ac confusi remanent cum partibus phlegmaticis, a quibus per actionem ignis faciliter separantur, et avolant; sicque per distillationem fit aqua vitæ, quæ aliud non est quam sulphur vini volatile cum tenuiore parte phlegmatis simul cum dicto sulphure vi ignis elevata. Post quadraginta dies, alia incipit vini fermentatio, quæ longiori, aut minus longo tempore perficitur, pro vini perfectiori, aut imperfectiori maturitate, et alio, atque alio modo terminatur, pro minore aut majore spiritus sulphurei abundantia. Si enim abundat in vino sulphur, acescit fermentatione, et evadit acetum; si autem parum sulphuris continet, lentescit vinum, et Italice dicitur* vino molle, *aut* vino guasto. *Quod si vinum maturum sit, ut cæteris paribus est, vinum dulce breviori tempore, aut acescit, aut lentescit, ut quotidiana constat experientia. In dicta autem fermentatione ordo essentialis partium vini mutatur; non enim ipsius quantitas, aut materia imminuitur, aut mutatur: videmus enim lagenam vino plenam tractu temporis evadere plenam aceto, nullatenus mutata circa quantitatem materiæ, quæ prius ibi extabat, sed tantum mutato partium essentiali ordine: nam sulphur, quod, ut diximus, erat phlegmati unitum, ac a tartaro separatum, iterum tartaro implicatur, et cum eo fixatur, et proinde si distilletur acetum, primo prodit phlegma insipidum, et post spiritus aceti, qui est sulphur vini illaqueatum particulis tartari minus fixi. Mutatio autem essentialis partium supradictarum variat substantiam liquoris expressi ab uva, quod manifeste patet ex variis, et contrariis effectibus, quos causant mustum, vinum, et acetum, et vinum lentum, quod vocatur corruptum, ut proinde duo prima apta materia sint ad consecrationem, secus alia duo. Hanc porro vini economiam hausimus ab erudito opere Nicolai Lemerii, Regis Galliarum Aromatarii,* Curs. de Chimi., p. 2. c. 9

56. Datam ergo naturalem doctrinam applicando consequenter dico, quod data dictorum animalium corporeitate subtili, et tenui, sicut corpora liquidorum, et data pariter eorundem organizatione et figuratione, quæ partium essentialem ordinationem exigunt, non sequerentur inconvenientia ex adverso illata: nam sicut (quemadmodum dicebamus) ex confusione partium vini, et diversa ipsarum accidentali positione non variatur ordinatio earumdem essentialis, ita esset in corpore tenui dictorum animalium.

57. Quinta interrogatio est, an talia obnoxia essent ægritudinibus, ac aliis imperfectionibus, quibus homines laborant, ut ignorantia, metu, segnitie, sensuum impedimentis, etc.? An laborando lassarentur, et ad virium reparationem egerent somno, cibo, ac potu, et quo? et consequenter an interirent, et subinde, an a cæteris animalibus casu, aut ruina possent occidi?

58. Respondeo, quod ex quo corpora ipsorum, quamvis tenuia, essent materiata, essent quidem corruptioni obnoxia; et ex consequenti possent pati ab agentibus contrariis, et ita ægrotare, puta, aut simpliciter, aut nisi ægre, perverse, aut vitiose præstare non posse munera, ad quæ eorum organa essent ordinata; in hoc siquidem consistit animalium quorumdam ægritudo quævis: ut resolutive docet præstantissimus Michael Ettmullerus, Physiol. c. 5., thes. 1. Verum est, quod ex eo, quod tantam materiæ crassitatem non haberent, et forte ex tot elementorum mixtione eorum corpus non constaret, et minus compositum esset, quam humanum, non tam facile paterentur a contrariis, et consequenter non tot ægritudinibus velut homines essent obnoxia, et longiorem, etiam homine, vitam ducerent: quo enim perfectius est animal, a tota specie, etiam cæteris, diutius vivit, ut patet de specie humana, cujus vita longior cæteris animalibus est. Nec enim admitto sæcularem vitam cornicum, cervorum, corvorum, et similium, de quibus more suo fabulatur Plinius, et ejus somnia sine prævia discussione secuti sunt cæteri: quandoquidem nullus est, qui talium animalium natale et interitum fideliter adnotaverit, ut pari modo de eo scripserit; sed insolitam diu fabulam quisque secutus est; sicut etiam illud, quod de Phœnice dicitur, quod ut quid fabulosum, circa ejus vitæ spatium recenset Tacitus, l. 6. Annal. Inferendum subinde esset quod illorum animalium vita etiam humana deberet esse diuturnior: ut enim infra dicemus, illa essent homine nobiliora, consequenter dicendum esset, quod essent obnoxia cæteris corporeis pathematis, et quiete, et cibo indigerent, quale diximus supra n° 50. Quia vero rationalia, et proinde disciplinabilia essent, ex consequenti etiam capacia ignorantiæ, si eorum ingenia non essent exculta studiis, et disciplina, et inter ea pro intellectus eorum majori, et minori acumine essent aliqua magis, aliqua minus in scientiis excellentia: universaliter vero, et a tota specie essent homine doctiora, non ob eorum corpoream subtilitatem, tum forte, ob majorem spirituum activitatem, tum ob diuturniorem vitæ durationem, in qua plura, quam homines discere possent, quas causas assignat D. Augustinus, lib. de Divin. Dæm. c. 3. init. tom. 3., et lib. de Spir. et Anima, *c. 37., pro futurorum prænotione in Dæmonibus. Ab agentibus autem naturalibus pati quidem pos-*

sent, ac difficulter occidi ratione velocitatis, qua possunt se subtrahere a nocentibus; quapropter, nec a brutis, nec ab homine armis naturalibus, seu artificialibus nisi maxima difficultate possent occidi, aut mutilari, et maxima eorumdem velocitate in declinando contrarium impetum. Possent vero in somno, aut in non advertentia occidi, et mutilari a corpore solido, ut ense vibrato ab homine, aut lapide delapso per ruinam, quia eorum corpus licet tenue, tamen et quantum, et divisibile esset, velut ær qui ferro, fuste, aut alio corpore solido dividitur quamvis tenuis sit. Eorum autem spiritus impartibilis esset, et ceu anima hominis totus in toto, et totus in quavis corporis parte. Hinc fieret quod diviso corpore ipsorum, ut præfertur, per aliud corpus, sequi posset mutilatio, et proinde etiam mors: non enim fieri posset ut diviso corpore idem spiritus utramque partem informaret, cum ipse indivisibilis esset. Verum est quod sicut partes æris divisæ, per intermedium corpus, hoc sublato iterum uniuntur, et evadit idem ær, possent pariter partes corporis divisæ, ut supra ponitur, reuniri, et ab eodem spiritu revivificari. Sed hoc modo nequirent talia animalia ab agentibus naturalibus, aut artificialibus occidi: sed rationabilior esset prima positio; ex hoc enim, quod communicarent cum cæteris in materia, æquum est, ut a cæteris, etiam usque ad eorum interitum pati possent, ut fit cum cæteris.

59. Sexta interrogatio est, an ipsorum corpora possent alia corpora penetrare, ut parietes, ligna, metalla, vitrum, etc., et an multa ipsorum possent in eodem loco materiali consistere, et ad quantum spatium extenderetur, seu restringeretur eorum corpus?

60. Respondeo, quod cum in omnibus corporibus quantumvis compactis dentur pori, ut ad sensum patet in metallis, de quibus major esset ratio, quod in ipsis non darentur pori: microscopio perfecte elaborato discernuntur pori metallorum, cum suis diversis figuris, utique possent per poros insinuari quibusvis corporibus, et hoc modo ista penetrare, quantumvis tales pori penetrari non possent ab alio liquore, aut spiritu materiali, aut vini, salis ammoniaci, aut similium, quia longe tenuiora essent istis liquoribus illorum corpora. Quamvis autem plures Angeli possint esse in eodem loco materiali, et etiam restringi ad locum minorem minore non tamen in infinitum, ut probat Scotus in 2. dist. 2. q. 6. § Ad proposi. et quæst. 8., per totum, hoc tamen concedendum non esset de corporibus talium animalium; tum quia corpora ipsa essent quanta, et eorum dimensio non esset reciproce penetrabilis; tum quia si duo corpora gloriosa non possunt esse in eodem loco, quamvis possint simul esse gloriosum, et non gloriosum, ut voluit Gotofredus

de Fontibus, quodlibet 6. q. 5., a quo non discordat Scotus in 2. distinct. 2. q. 8. in fine; multo minus possent simul esse istorum corpora, quæ, licet subtilia, non tamen æquarent subtilitatem corporis gloriosi. Quo autem ad extensionem, et restrictionem dicendum esset, quod sicut ex rarefactione, et condensatione majus, aut minus spatium occupatur ab ære, qui etiam arte potest constringi, ut in minori loco contineatur, quam sit suæ quantitati naturaliter debitus, ut patet in magnis pilis lusoriis, quæ per fistulam seu tubum inflatorium inflantur: in his siquidem ær violenter immittitur, et constringitur, et ejus major ibi continetur quantitas, quam naturalis pilæ capacitas exigat; ita pariformiter talia corpora ex ipsorum naturali virtute possent ad majus spatium non tamen excedens eorumdem quantitatem, extendi: ut pariter etiam restringi, non tamen circa determinatum locum suæ quantitati debitum. Et quia ipsorum nonnulla prout etiam in hominibus est, essent magna, et nonnulla parva, congruum esset, ut magna possent plus extendi, quam parva et hæc ad minorem locum restringi, quam magna.

61. *Septima interrogatio est, an hujusmodi animalia in peccato originali nascerentur, et a Christo Domino fuissent redempta; an ipsis conferretur gratia, et per quæ sacramenta; sub qua lege viverent, et an Beatitudinis, et Damnationis essent capacia?*

62. *Respondeo, quod articulus Fidei est, quod Christus Dominus pro universa creatura rationali gratiam, et gloriam meruit. Pariter articulus Fidei est, quod Creaturæ rationali gloria non confertur nisi præcedat in ea gratia, quæ est dispositio ad gloriam. Similis articulus est quod gloria non confertur nisi per merita. Hæc vero fundantur in observantia perfecta mandatorum Dei adimpleta per gratiam. Ex his satis fit positis interrogationibus. Incertum est an tales Creaturæ originaliter peccavissent, necne. Certum tamen est, quod si ipsarum Prothoparens peccasset, sicut peccavit Adam, ipsius descendentes in peccato originali nascerentur, quemadmodum nascuntur homines. Et quia Deus nunquam reliquit Creaturam rationalem sine remedio, dum ipsa est in via; si hujusmodi creaturæ in peccato originali, aut actuali inficerentur, Deus providisset illis de remedio, sed quale sit, an fecisset, noverit Deus, noverint ipsæ. Hoc certum est si inter ipsas essent eadem, aut alia Sacramenta, ac sunt in Ecclesia humana militanti, ipsa habuissent, et institutionem, et efficaciam a meritis Jesu Christi, qui omnium creaturarum rationalium Redemptor, et Satisfactor universalis est. Convenientissimum pariter,*

immo necessarium esset quod sub aliqua lege a Deo sibi data viverent, ut per ipsius observantiam possent sibi beatitudinem mereri; quænam autem lex fuisset, an naturalis tantum, aut scripta, Mosaica, aut Evangelica, aut alia ab his omnibus differens, prout Deo placuisset, hoc nobis incognitum. Quoquomodo autem fuisset, nulla resultaret repugnantia possibilitatem talium creaturarum excludens.

63. Unicum porro argumentum, et quidem satis debile post longam meditationem mihi subit contra talium creaturarum possibilitatem: et est quod si tales creaturæ in Mundo existerent, de ipsis notitia aliqua tradita fuisset a Philosophis, Sacra Scriptura, Traditione Ecclesiastica, aut Sanctis Patribus; quod cum non fuerit, tales creaturas minime possibiles esse concludendum est.

64. Sed hoc argumentum, quod revera magis pulsat existentiam, quam possibilitatem illarum, facili negotio solvitur ex iis quæ præmissimus supra n⁰ 41. et 42. Argumentum enim ab auctoritate negativa non tenet. Præterquam quod falsum est, quod de illis notitiam non tradiderint tum Philosophi, tum Scriptura, tum Patres. Plato siquidem, ut refert Apuleius de Deo Socratis et Plutarchus de Isid. apud Baronem, Scot. Defens., *tom. 9.* Apparat. p. 1. fol. 2., voluit Dæmones esse animalia genere, animo passiva, mente rationalia, corpore ærea, tempore æterna: creaturasque istas nomine Dæmonum*intitulavit; quod tamen nomen non male sonat ex se: importat enim plenum sapientia; unde cum Diabolum (Angelum nempe malum) volunt auctores exprimere, non simpliciter Dæmonem, sed* Cacodæmonem*vocant: sicut Eudæmonem, quando bonum Angelum volunt intelligi. Similiter in Scriptura Sacra et Patribus, de dictis creaturis habetur mentio, et de hoc infra dicemus.*

65. Stabilita huc usque talium creaturarum possibilitate, ad earumdem existentiam probandam descendamus. Supposita tot historiarum veritate de coitu hujusmodi Incuborum et Succuborum cum hominibus et brutis, ita ut hoc negare impudentia videatur, ut ait D. Augustinus quem dedimus, supra n⁰ 10., ita arguo: Ubi reperitur propria passio sensus, ibidem necessario reperitur sensus ipse, cum juxta principia philosophica propria passio fluat a natura, sive ubi reperiuntur actiones, seu operationes sensus, ibidem reperitur sensus ipse, cum operationes et actiones sint a forma. Atqui in hujusmodi Incubis aut Succubis, sunt actiones, operationes, ac propriæ passiones, quæ sunt a sensibus; ergo in iisdem reperitur sensus: sed sensus reperiri nequit nisi adsint organa composita, nempe ex potentia animæ et determinata parte corporis: ergo in iisdem reperiuntur corpus et anima; erunt igitur animalia: sed etiam in ipsis et ab ipsis sunt actiones, et operationes animæ rationalis: ergo eorum anima erit rationalis: et ita de primo ad ultimum tales Incubi sunt animalia rationalia.

66. *Minor probatur quoad singulas ejus partes. Passio siquidem appetitiva coitus est passio sensus; mœror, ac tristitia, ac iracundia et furor ex coitu denegato passiones sensus sunt, ut patet in quibusvis animalibus; generatio per coitum est operatio sensus, ut notum est. Hæc porro omnia in Incubis sunt, ut enim probavimus supra a n° 25. et seq.;* ipsi coitum muliebrem, et quandoque virilem appetunt, tristantur, et furunt, ut amantes, amentes, si ipsis denegetur; coeunt perfecte et quandoque generant. Concludendum ergo quod polleant sensu, et proinde corpore; unde inferendum etiam perfecta animalia esse. Pariter clausis ostiis ac fenestris intrant ubivis locorum: igitur ipsorum corpus *tenue est; item futura prænoscunt, annuntiant, componunt, ac dividunt; quæ operationes sunt propriæ animæ rationalis: ergo anima rationali pollent; et ita sunt vera animalia rationalia. Respondent communiter Doctores, quod malus Dæmon est ille qui tales impudicitias operatur, quod passiones, nempe amorem, tristitiamque simulat ex coitu denegato, ut animas ad peccandum alliciat, et eas perdat; et si coit, et generat, hoc est ex semine, et in corpore alieno, ut dictum fuit supra n° 24.*

67. *Sed contra Incubi nonnulli rem habent cum equis, equabus, aliisque etiam brutis, quæ si coitum adversentur, male ab ipsis tractantur, ut quotidiana constat experientia; sed in istis cessat ratio adducta, nempe quod fingat appetitum coitus, ut animas perdat, cum anima brutorum damnationis æternæ sit incapax. Præterea amoris et iræ passiones in ipso contrarios effectus reales producunt. Si enim aut mulier aut brutum amatum illis morem gerant, optime ab Incubis tractantur; viceversa pessime habentur, si ex denegato coitu irascantur et furant; et hoc firmatur quotidiana experientia; ergo in ipsis sunt veræ passiones sensus. Insuper mali Dæmones, ac incorporei, qui rem habent cum Sagis et Maleficis, ipsas cogunt ad eorum adorationem, ad denegandam Fidem Orthodoxam, ad maleficia et scelera enormia perpetranda tanquam pensum infamis coitus, ut supra n° 11. dictum fuit:* nihil horum prætendunt Incubi, ergo mali Dæmones non sunt. Ulterius malus Dæmon, ut ex Peltano et Thyreo scribit Guaccius, Compend. Malef. lib. 1. c. 19. fol. 128., ad prolationem nominis Jesu aut Mariæ, ad formationem signi Crucis, ad approximationem sacrarum Reliquiarum, sive rerum benedictarum,

et ad exorcismos, adjurationes, aut præcepta sacerdotum, aut fugit aut pavet, concutiturque, et stridet, ut conspicitur quotidie in energumenis, et constat ex tot historiis, quas recitat Guaccius, ex quibus habetur, quod in nocturnis ludis Sagarum facto ab aliquo assistentium signo Crucis, aut pronuntiato nomine Jesu, Diaboli et secum Sagæ omnes disparuerunt. Sed Incubi ad supradicta nec fugiunt, nec pavent, quandoque cachinnis exorcismos excipiunt, et quandoque ipsos Exorcistas cædunt, et sacras vestes discerpunt. Quod si mali Dæmones, utpote a D. N. J. C. domiti, ad ipsius nomen, Crucem, et res sacras pavent: boni autem Angeli eisdem rebus gaudent, non tamen homines ad peccata et Dei offensam sollicitant: Incubi vero sacra non timent, et ad peccata provocant, convincitur ipsos nec malos Dæmones, nec bonos Angelos esse; sed patet, quod nec homines sunt, cum tamen ratione utantur. Quid ergo erunt? Si in termino sunt, et simplices spiritus sunt, erunt aut damnati aut beati: non enim in bona Theologia dantur puri spiritus viatores. Si damnati, nomen et Crucem Christi revererentur; si beati, homines ad peccandum non provocarent; ergo aliud erunt a puris spiritibus; et sic erunt corporati, et viatores.

68. Præterea agens materiale non potest agere nisi in passum similiter materiale; tritum siquidem est axioma philosophorum, quod agens, et patiens debent communicare in subjecto; nec id quod materiatum est, potest agere in rem pure spiritualem. Dantur autem agentia naturalia, quæ agunt contra hujusmodi Dæmones Incubos; sequitur igitur quod isti materiati, seu corporei sunt. Minor probatur ex iis quæ scribunt Dioscorides, l. 2. c. 168. et l. 1. c. 100., Plinius, lib. 15. c. 4., Aristoteles, Probl. 34., et Apuleius, l. De Virtute Herbarum, apud Guaccium, Comp. Malef., l. 3. c. 13. fol. 316., et confirmatur experientia, nempe de pluribus herbis, lapidibus ac animalibus, quæ Dæmones depellunt, ut ruta, hypericon, verbena, scordium, palma Christi, centaureum, adamas, corallium, gagates, jaspis, pellis capitis lupi aut asini, menstruum muliebre, et centum alia; unde habetur 26, q. 7. cap. final.: Dæmonium sustinenti liceat petras, vel herbas habere sine incantatione. Ex quo habetur, petras aut herbas posse sua vi naturali Dæmonis vires compescere, aliter Canon hoc non permitteret, sed ut superstitiosum vetaret. Et de hoc luculentum exemplum habemus in Sacra Scriptura, ubi Angelus Raphael dixit Tobiæ, c. 6. v. 8.: cordis ejus (nempe piscis, quem a Tigri attraxerat) particulam, si super carbones ponas, fumus ejus extricat omne genus Dæmoniorum. *Et ejus virtutem experientia comprobavit: nam incenso jecore piscis, fugatus est Incubus, qui Saram deperiebat.*

69. Respondent ad hæc communiter Theologi, quod talia agentia naturalia in-choative tantum fugant Dæmonem, completive autem vis supernaturalis Dei aut Angeli, ita ut virtus supernaturalis sit causa primaria, directa, et principalis, naturalis autem secondaria, indirecta, et minus principalis. Unde ab probationem, quæ supra adducta est de Dæmone fugato a fumo jecoris piscis incensi a Tobia, respondet Vallesius, De Sac. Philosoph., c. 28., quod tali fumo indita fuit a Deo vis supernaturalis fugandi Incubum, sicut igni materiali Inferni data est virtus torquendi Dæmones et animas Damnatorum. Ad eamdem autem probationem respondet Lyranus, et Cornelius ad c. 6. Tob. v. 8., Abulentis in 1. Reg. c. 16. q. 46., Pererius in Daniel., pag. 272., apud Cornel. loc. cit., fumum cordis piscis expulisse Dæmonem inchoate vi naturali, sed complete vi angelica et cœlesti: naturali autem impediendo actionem Dæmonis per dispositionem contrariam, quia hic agit per naturales causas et humores, quorum qualitates expugnantur a qualitatibus contrariis rerum naturalium, quæ dicuntur Dæmones fugare; et in eadem sententia sunt omnes loquentes de arte exorcista.

70. Sed hæc responsio, que tamen validas habet instantias, ad plus quadrare po-test contra malos Dæmones obsidentes corpora, aut per maleficia inferentes ipsis ægritudines, aut alia incommoda, sed nullo modo facit ad propositum de Incubis: siquidem isti nec corpora obsident, nec ipsis officiunt per ægritudines habituales, sed ad plus ictibus et percussionibus torquent. Quod si equas coitum adversantes macras reddunt, hoc faciunt subducendo illis cibum, et hoc modo macrescere, et tandem interire eas faciunt. Ad hæc autem patranda non eget Incubus alicujus rei naturalis applicatione (qua tamen eget malus Dæmon inferens ægritudinem habitualem), ea enim potest ex sua vi organica naturali. Pariter Dæmon malus plerumque obsidet corpora, et infert ægritudines ad signa cum ipso conventa et posita a Saga aut Malefico, quæ signa multoties res naturales sunt, præditæ vi nativa nocendi, quibus naturaliter resistunt alia pariter naturalia contrariæ vir-tutis. Incubus vero non sic; quia ex se, et nulla concurrente aut Saga aut Malefico, suas vexationes infert. Præterea res naturales fugantes Incubos suam virtutem exercent, ac effectum sortiuntur absque interventu alicujus exorcismi aut sacræ benedictionis; ut proinde dici non possit, quod fuga Incubi inchoative sit a virtute naturali, completive autem a vi divina, quia ibi nulla particularis intervenit divini nominis invocatio, sed est purus effectus rei naturalis, ad quem non concurrit Deus, nisi concursu universali, tanquam auctor naturæ, et causa universalis, et prima in ordine efficientium.

71. Duas circa hoc historias do, quarum primam habui a Confessario Monialium, viro gravi, ac fide dignissimo. Alterius vero sum testis oculatus.

In quodam Sanctimonialium monasterio degebat ad educationem Virgo quædam nobilis tentata ab Incubo, qui diu noctuque ipsi apparebat, ipsam ad coitum sollicitando eniximis precibus, tamquam amasius præ amore dementatus; ipsa tamen semper restitit tentanti gratia Dei, ac sacramentorum frequentia roborata. Incassum abiere plures devotiones, jejunia et vota facta a puella vexata, exorcismi, benedictiones, et præcepta ab exorcistis facta Incubo, ut desisteret a molestia illa; nec quidquam proficiebatur multitudo reliquiarum, aliarumque rerum benedictarum disposita in camera virginis tentatæ, nec benedictæ candelæ noctu ibidem ardentes impediebant, quominus juxta consuetum appareret ad tentandum in forma speciosissimi juvenis. Consultas inter alios viros doctos fuit quidam Theologus magnæ eruditionis: iste advertens virginem tentatam esse temperamenti phlegmatici a toto, conjectavit Incubum esse dæmonem aqueum (dantur enim ut scribit Guaccius, Comp. Malefic. l. 1. c. 19. fol. 129., Dæmones ignei, ærei, phlegmatici, terrei, subterranei, et lucifugi), et consuluit quod in camera virginis tentatæ continue fieret suffimentum vaporosum sequens. Requirunt ollam novam figulinam vitreatam; in hac ponitur calami aromatici, cubebarum seminis, aristolochiæ utriusque radicum, cardamomi majoris et minoris, gingiberis, piperis longi, caryophyllorum, cinnamomi, canellæ caryophyllatæ, macis, nucum myristicarum, styracis calamitæ, benzoini, ligni ac radicis rodiæ, ligni aloes, triasantalorum una uncia, semiaquæ vitæ libræ tres; ponitur olla supra cineres calidas ut vapor suffimenti ascendat, et cella clausa tenetur. Facto suffimento advenit denuo Incubus, sed ingredi cellam nunquam ausus est: sed si tentata extra eam ibat, et per viridarium ac claustra spatiabatur, aliis invisibilis sibi visus apparebat Incubus, et puellæ *collo injectis brachiis violenter, ac quasi furtive oscula rapiebat: quod molestissimum honestæ virgini erat. Consultus denuo Theologus ille ordinavit puellæ, ut deferret pixidulas unguentarias exquisitorum odorum, ut moschi, ambræ, zibetti, balsami Peruviani, ac aliorum compositorum; quod cum fecisset, deambulanti per viridarium puellæ apparuit Incubus faci minaci, ac furenti; non tamen ad illam approximavit, sed digitum sibi momordit tanquam meditans vindictam; tandem disparuit, nec amplius ab ea visus fuit.*

72. Alia historia est, quod in Conventu Magnæ Cartusiæ Ticinensis, fuit quidam Diaconus, nomine dictus Augustinus, maximas, ac inauditas, et pene incredibiles sustinens a quodam Dæmone vexationes; quæ tolli nullo remedio spirituali (quamvis plura juxta plures exorcistas, qui liberationem, sed incassum tentarunt, fuissent adhibita) potuerunt. Me consuluit illius Conventus vicarius, qui curam divexati, utpote Clerici ex officio habebat. Ego videns frustranea fuisse consueta exorcismorum remedia, exemplo historiæ suprarecensitæ consului suffimentum simile superiori, utque divexatus pixidulas odoramentorum supradictas deferret; et quia tabacchi usum habebat, et aqua vitæ delectabatur, suasi, ut et tabaccho et aqua vitæ moschata uteretur. Dæmon illi apparebat diu, noctuque ultra alias species, puta scheleti, suis, asini, Angeli, avis, modo in forma unius, modo alterius ex suis Religiosis, et semel in forma sui Prælati, nempe Prioris, qui hortatus est vexatum ad puritatem conscientiæ, ad confidentiam in Deum, et ad frequentiam confessionis; suasit ut sibi sacramentalem confessionem faceret, quod etiam fecit; et expost Psalmos Exsurgat Deus *et* Qui habitat, *et mox Evangelium S. Joannis simul cum vexato recitavit, et ad ea verba* Verbum caro factum est *genuflexit, et accepta stola, quæ in cella erat, et aspergillo aquæ benedictæ benedixit cellæ, ac lecto vexati, et ac si revera fuisset ipsius Prior præceptum fecit Dæmoni, ne auderet illum suum subditum amplius divexare, et post hæc disparuit, sicque prodidit quisnam esset: aliter vexatus illum suum Prælatum esse reputaverat. Postquam igitur suffimentum, ac odores, ut supra dictum est, consulueram, non destitit Dæmon juxta solitum apparere; imo assumpta figura vexati fuit ad cameram Vicarii, et ab eo petiit aquam vitæ, ac tabaccum moschatum, dicens sibi talia valde placere. Vicarius utrumque illi dedit: quibus acceptis disparuit in momento, quo facto cognovit Vicarius se fuisse illusum a Dæmone tali pacto: quod magis confirmavit assertum vexati, qui cum juramento affirmavit, se illa die nullo modo fuisse in cella Vicarii. Iste mihi totum retulit, et ex tali facto conjeci Dæmonem illum non fuisse aqueum, ut erat Incubus, qui virginem ad coitum sollicitabat, ut dictum supra est, sed igneum, vel ad minus æreum, ex quo gaudebat vaporibus, ac odoribus, tabacco, et aqua vitæ, quæ calida sunt. Et conjecturæ vim addidit temperamentum divexati, quod erat colericum quo ad prædominium cum subdominio, tamen sanguineo. Dæmones enim tales non accedunt nisi ad eos, qui secum in temperamento symbolizant; ex quo validatur opinio mea de illorum corporeitate. Unde suasi Vicario, ut acciperet herbas natura frigidas, ut nymphæam, hepaticam, portulacam, mandragoram, sempervivam, plantaginem, hyoscyamum, et alias similes, et ex iis compositum fasciculum fenestræ, alium ostio cellæ suspenderet; similibusque herbis, tum cameram, tum lectum divexati sterneret. Mirum dictu! comparuit denuo Dæmon, manens tamen extra cameram, nec ingredi voluit, et cum divexatus illum interrogasset, quare de more intrare non auderet, multis verbis injuriosis jactatis*

contra me, qui talia consulueram, disparuit, nec amplius reversus est.

73. Ex his duabus historiis apparet tales odores, et herbas respective sua naturali virtute, nullaque interveniente vi supernaturali Dæmones propulisse; unde convincitur quod Incubi patiuntur a qualitatibus materialibus, ut proinde concludi debeat, quod communicant in materia cum iis rebus naturalibus, a quibus fugantur, et ex consequenti corpore sint præditi, quod est intentum.

74. Et magis conclusio firmatur, si impugnetur sententia Doctorum supracitatorum, dicentium, Incubum abactum a Sara fuisse vi Angeli Raphaelis, non vero jecoris piscis callionymi, qualis fuit piscis a Tobia apprehensus ad ripam Tigris, ut cum Vallesio, Sacr. Philos., *c. 42., scribit Cornelius a Lap.* in Tob. *c. 6., v. 2.,* § Quarto ergo: *salva enim tantorum Doctorum reverentia, talis expositio manifeste adversatur sensui patenti Textus, a quo nullo modo recedendum est dummodo non sequantur absurda. En verba Angeli ad Tobiam:* «Cordis ejus particulam, si super carbones ponas, fumus ejus extricat omne genus Dæmoniorum, sive a viro, sive a muliere, ita ut ultra non accedant ad eos, et fel valet ad unguendos oculos, in quibus fuerit albugo, et sanabuntur.» (Tob., *c. 6. v. 8. et 9.) Notetur, quæso, assertio Angeli absoluta, et universalis de virtute cordis, seu jecoris, et fellis illius piscis: non enim dicit:* Si pones particulas cordis ejus super carbones, fugabis omne genus Dæmoniorum, et si felle unges oculos, in quibus fuerit albugo, sanabuntur: *si enim ita dixisset congrua esset expositio, quod nempe Raphael supernaturali sua virtute illos effectus patrasset, ad quos perficiendos inepta esset applicatio fumi, et fellis: sed non ita loquitur, sed ait talem esse virtutem fumi, et fellis absolute.*

75. Quæro modo, an Angelus veritatem puram dixerit de virtute rerum, an mentiri potuerit; pariter an albugo ab oculis Tobiæ senioris ablata sit vi naturali fellis piscis, aut virtute supernaturali Angeli Raphaelis? Angelum mentiri potuisse blasphemia hæreticalis est; sequitur igitur puram veritatem fuisse ab eo assertam; talis autem non esset, si omne genus Dæmoniorum non extricaretur a fumo jecoris piscis nisi addita vi supernaturali Angeli, maxime, si hæc esset causa principalis talis effectus, quemadmodum scribunt de hoc casu Doctores. Mentiretur absque dubio medicus qui diceret, talis herba curat taliter pleuritidem, sive epilepsiam, ut amplius non revertatur: si herba illa non curaret illas ægritudines nisi inchoate, et perfecta illarum sanatio esset ab alia herba conjuncta priori; sic pari modo mentitus fuisset Raphael asserens fumum jecoris extricare omne genus Dæmoniorum ita ut ultra

non accedant, si talis effectus esset a fumo solum inchoate, principaliter vero, et
perfecte a virtute Angeli. Praeterea talis fuga Daemonis, vel secutura erat univer-
saliter, et semper posito jecore piscis super carbones a quoquam, vel debebat sequi
in illo solummodo casu particulari, jecore incusso a juniore Tobia. Si primum,
ergo oportet, quod cuicumque talem fumum per accensionem jecoris paranti, as-
sistat Angelus qui supernaturali virtute Daemonem miraculose abigat regulariter;
et hoc est absurdum; ad positionem enim rei naturalis deberet regulariter sequi
miraculum, quod est incongruum, et si absque Angeli operatione fuga Daemonis
non sequeretur, mentitus fuisset Raphael asserens eam esse virtutem jecoris. Si
autem effectus ille sequi non debeat, nisi in illo casu particulari, mentitus fuisset
Angelus enuncians universaliter virtutem piscis, in fugando omni Daemoniorum
genere, quod non est dicendum.

76. *Ulterius albugo oculorum detracta est ab oculis Tobiae senioris, et ipsius caecitas*
sanata est a virtute naturali fellis piscis illius, ut Doctores affirmant (Liran. Dyoni-
sius; et Seraci. apud Cornel. in Tobi., *c. 6. v. 9). Piscis enim Callionymus, qui voca-*
tur Italice bocca in capo, *et quo usus est Tobias, fel habet pro celeberrimo remedio*
ad detegendas albugines oculorum, ut scribunt concorditer Dioscorides, l. 1. c. 96.,
Galenus, De Simpl. Medicam., *Plinius, l. 32. c. 7.,* Aclanius, De Ver. Histor., *l. 13.*
c. 14. et Vallesius, De Sacr. Philos., *c. 47. Textus Graecus* Tobiae, *c. 11. v. 13., habet:*
«Inspersit fel super oculos patris sui, dicens: Confide, Pater; ut autem erosi sunt,
detrivit oculos suos, et disquamatae sunt ab angulis oculorum albugines.» Cum
igitur eodem contextu Angelus aperuerit Tobiae virtutem jecoris, et fellis piscis, et
hoc sua naturali virtute caecitatem Tobiae senioris curaverit, concludendum est,
quod etiam fumus jecoris sua naturali vi Incubum fugaverit: quod concludenter
confirmatur a Textu Graeco, qui ad Tobiae c. 8. v. 2., ubi Vulgata habet: «Partem
jecoris posuit super carbones vivos», sic habet: «Accepit cinerem, sive prunam
thimiamatum, et imposuit cor piscis, et hepar, fumumque fecit, et quando
odoratus est Daemon odores, fugit.» Et Textus Hebraicus ita cantat: «Percepit
Asmodeus odorem, et fugit.» Ex quibus textibus apparet, quod Daemon fugit
ad perceptionem fumi, sibi contrarii, ac nocentis, non autem a virtute Angeli
supernaturali. *Quod si in tali liberatione Sarae ab impetitione Incubi Asmodei,*
ultra fumum jecoris intervenit operatio Raphaelis, hoc fuit in alligatione Daemo-
nis in deserto superioris Ægypti, ut dicitur c. 8. v. 3. Tobiae; fumus quippe jecoris
nequibat in tanta distantia agere in Daemonem, aut illum alligare. Quod inservire
potest pro concordia supracitatorum Doctorum (qui voluerunt Saram perfecte

liberatam a Dæmone virtute Raphaelis) cum sententia, quam tuemur: dico enim,
quod ipsi senserint, quod perfecta curatio Saræ a Dæmone fuerit in alligatione ejus
in deserto, quæ fuit ab Angelo, quod et nos concedimus; sed extricatio, sive fugatio
ejusdem a cubiculo Saræ fuerit a vi innativa jecoris piscis, quod nos tuemur.

77. Probatur tertio principaliter nostra conclusio de existentia talium animalium,
seu de Incuborum corporeitate, ex auctoritate D. Hieronymi, in vita S. Pauli primi
Eremitæ. *Refert is D. Antonium iter per desertum arripuisse, ut ad visendum D.*
Paulum perveniret, et post nonnullas diætas itineris Centaurum reperiisse, a quo
cum fuisset percontatus mansionem D. Pauli, et ille barbarum quid infrendens
potius, quam proloquens, dextræ protensione manus iter D. Antonio demonstras-
set, in sylvam se abdidit cursu concitatissimo. Prosecutus iter S. Abbas in quadam
valle invenit haud grandem quemdam homunculum, aduncis manibus, fronte
cornibus asperata, cujus extrema pars corporis in caprarum pedes desinebat. Ad
ejus aspectum substitit Antonius, et timens Diaboli artes signo Sanctæ Crucis se
munivit. Ad tale signum nec fugit, nec metuit homuncio ille, immo ad sanctum se-
nem actu humili appropinquans palmarum fructus ad viaticum quasi pacis obsides
illi offerebat. Tum B. *Antonius quisnam esset interrogans, hoc ab eo responsum*
accepit: «Mortalis ego sum, et unus ex accolis Eremi, quos vario errore delusa
Gentilitas Faunos, Satyros, et Incubos vocans colit; legatione fungor gregis mei;
precamur, ut pro nobis communem Deum depreceris, quem pro salute mundi
venisse cognovimus, et universam terram exiit sonus ejus.» Ad quæ gaudens
D. Antonius de gloria Christi, conversus ad Alexandriam, et baculo terram
percutiens, ait: «Veh tibi, Civitas meretrix, quæ pro diis animalia veneraris!»
Hæc D. Hieronymus, qui late prosequitur hoc factum, ipsius virtutem longo
comprobans sermone.

78. De hujus historiæ veritate dubitare temerarium est, cum eam constanter re-
ferat SS. Ecclesiæ Doctorum maximus D. Hieronymus, de cujus auctoritate nullus
Catholicus dubitabit. Addit fol. 21. 25.Notandæ proinde veniunt illius circum-
stantiæ, quæ sententiam nostram evidentissime confirmant.

79. Primo notandum est, quod si ullus Sanctorum artibus Dæmonis impetitus fuit;
si ullus diversas ejus artes nocendi calluit; si ullus victorias, ac illustria de eodem
trophea reportavit, is fuit D. Antonius, ut constat ex ejus vita a D. Athanasio
descripta. Dum igitur D. Antonius homunculum illum non tanquam Diabolum

agnovit, sed animal intitulavit dicens: Veh tibi, Civitas meretrix, quæ pro Diis animalia veneraris!*convincitur, quod ille nullo modo fuit Diabolus, seu purus spiritus de cœlo dejectus, ac damnatus, sed aliquod aliud animal. Et confirmatur, quia D. Antonius erudiens suos monachos, eosque animans ad metuendas Dæmonis violentias, aiebat, prout habetur in lectionibus Breviarii Romani in festo* S. Antonii Abb. l. l., quæ recitantur in festo ipsius: «Mihi credite, Fratres, pertimescit Satanas piorum vigilias, orationes, jejunia, voluntariam paupertatem, misericordiam, et humilitatem; maxime vero ardentem amorem in Christum Dominum, cujus unico Sanctissimæ Crucis signo debilitatus fugit.» Dum igitur homunculus ille, contra quem D. Antonius Crucis signo se munivit, ad ejus aspectum, nec pavit, nec fugit, immo confidenter, humiliterque accessit ad eum dactalos illi offerens, signum est, illum nullo modo Diabolum fuisse.

80. *Secundo notandum, quod homunculus ille dixit:* Mortalis et ego sum; ex quibus verbis docemur, quod ille erat animal morti obnoxium, et proinde, quod per generationem esse accepit: spiritus enim immaterialis immortalis est, quia simplex, et ideo non accipit esse per generationem ex præjacente materia, sed per creationem; unde nec amittit esse per corruptionem, quæ dicitur mors, sed per annihilationem tantum potest desinere esse. *Quod si ille se mortalem esse dixit, professus est se esse animal.*

81. *Tertio notandum, quod ait se cognovisse communem Deum in carne humana fuisse passum. Ex his verbis convincitur illud fuisse animal rationale: siquidem bruta nihil agnoscunt, nisi sensibile et præsens, unde ab ipsis Deus nullo modo cognosci potest. Quod si homunculus ille ait, se cum aliis suis cognovisse Deum in carne humana passum, hoc probat, quod aliquo revelante habuit notitiam de Deo, sicut etiam nos habemus de illo fidem revelatam; pariterque Deum carnem humanam assumpsisse, et in ea passum: quæ duo sunt articuli nostræ Fidei principales, nempe Dei unius, et Trini existentia, et ipsius Incarnatio, Passio, et Resurrectio; ex quibus omnibus habetur, ut dicebam, illud fuisse animal rationale capax divinæ cognitionis, per revelationem, ut nos, et proinde pollens anima rationali, et ex consequenti immortali.*

82. *Quarto notandum, quod oraverit nomine omnium gregis sui, cujus legatione fungi se profitebatur, D. Antonium, ut communem Deum pro illis deprecaretur. Ex his deducitur, quod homunculus ille capax erat beatitudinis, et damnationis,*

et quod non erat in termino, sed in via: ex hoc enim, quod, ut supra probatum est, se prodidit rationalem, et anima immortali consequenter donatum, consequens est, quod, et beatitudinis, et damnationis capax sit: hæc enim propria passio est Creaturæ rationalis, ut constat ex natura angelica, et humana. Item deducitur, quod ipse erat in via, et proinde capax meriti, et demeriti: si enim fuisset in termino, fuisset vel beatus, vel damnatus; neutrum autem potuit esse, quia orationes D. Antonii, quibus se commendabat, ipsi nullo modo prodesse potuissent, si fuisset finaliter damnatus; et si beatus fuisset illis non eguisset. Quod ipsi se commendavit, signum est eas sibi prodesse potuisse, et proinde in statu viæ, et meriti.

83. Quinto notandum, quod homunculus ille professus est, se esse legatum aliorum suæ speciei, dum dixit legatione fungor gregis mei, ex quibus verbis plura deducuntur. Unum est, quod homunculus ille non solus erat, unde potuisset credi monstrum raro contingens, sed quod plures erant ejusdem speciei; tum quia simul congregati gregem faciebant; tum quia nomine omnium veniebat: quod esse non posset si multorum voluntates in illum non convenissent. Aliud est, quod isti profitentur vitam socialem: ex quo nomine multorum unus ex ipsis missus est. Aliud est, quod quamvis dicantur habitare in Eremo, non tamen in eo fixa est eorum permanentia: siquidem cum D. Antonius in illa eremo alias non fuisset (distabat enim illa per multas dietas ab eremo D. Antonii), scire non potuerunt quisnam ille esset cujusve sanctitatis; necessarium igitur fuit, quod alibi eum cognoverint, et ex consequenti extra desertum illum vagaverint.

84. Ultimo notandum, quod homunculus ille ait esse ex iis, quos cæco errore delusa Gentilitas Faunos, Satyros et Incubos appellant; et ex his verbis convincitur nostrum intentum principale, Incubos nempe esse animalia rationalia beatitatis, et damnationis capacia.

85. Talium homuncionum frequens est apparitio in metallorum fodinis, ut scribit Gregorius Agricola, lib. De Animal. subterran., prope finem. Isti nempe coram fossoribus minerarum comparent induti habitu, qualem habent fossores ipsi, et jocantur inter se, tripudiantque, ac rident et cachinnantur, parvosque lapides joco mittunt in metallarios, et tunc signum est, ait Auctor prædictus, optimi proventus, ac inventionis alicujus rami, aut trunci principalis arboris mineralis.

86. Tales homunculos subterraneos negat Petrus Thyræus Novesianus, lib. De

Terrificatio. Noctur., *c. 2.*, per totum, *nixus argumentis sane puerilibus, quæ sunt hæc: si darentur hujusmodi homunciones, ubinam degunt, et quænam, et ubi habent sua domicilia, qua ratione genus suum conservant, si per generationem, aut quomodo? si oriantur, et intereant, quo cibo vitam suam sustentent; si beatitudinis, et damnationis capaces sunt, et quibus mediis propriam salutem consequantur? Hæc sunt argumenta Thyræi, quibus permotus negat talem existentiam.*

87. Sed viri parum cordati est negare id, quod graves Aucthores, fideque digni scribunt, quodque quotidiana constat experientia. Argumenta Thyræi nec minimum cogunt, ac ea solvimus supra a n° 45. et seq. Remanet solum satisfacere quæstioni ubinam locorum habitent hujusmodi homunculi, seu Incubi? Ad quod dico, quod ut supra dedimus n° 71. ex Guaccio, istorum alii sunt terrei, alii aquei, alii ærei, alii ignei, quorum nempe corpora, aut constant ex talium elementorum subtiliori parte, sive licet ex pluribus constent elementis, prævalet tamen in iis, aut aqua, aut ær pro ipsorum natura. Mansiones igitur, et domicilia eorum erunt in elemento illo cujus natura in eorum corporibus prævalet: ignei enim nisi violenter, et forte nullomodo in aquis aut locis palustribus morabuntur, cum hæc sint sibi contraria, nec aquei ad superiorem ætheris partem ascendere poterunt ob sibi *repugnantem regionis illius subtilitatem, quod etiam videmus accidere hominibus, qui ad quorumdam Alpium summa juga pervenire nequeunt præ summa æris subtilitate, quæ homines crassiori æri assuetos nutrire nequit.*

88. Pluribus sanctorum Patrum auctoritatibus, quas congerit Molina in p. p. D. Thom., q. 50., ar. 1. circa med., probare possemus Dæmonum corporeitatem; quæ tamen stante determinatione Concilii Lateranensis de incorporeitate Angelorum, ut dictum fuit supra n° 37., exponi debent de Dæmonibus istis Incubis, ac viatoribus adhuc, non autem de Damnatis. Tamen ne nimis longus sim, solius D. Augustini, summi Ecclesiæ Doctoris, authoritates damus, quibus evidenter convincitur illum fuisse in sententia, quam nos docemus.

89. D. Augustinus igitur, lib. 2. super Genesim ad litteram c. 17. de Dæmonibus, *sic habet:* «Quædam vera nosse, partim quia subtiliore sensus acumine, partim quia subtilioribus corporibus vigent,» et lib. 3. c. 1., «etsi Dæmones ærea sunt animalia, quoniam corporum æreorum natura vigent.» Et Epistola 115. ad Hebridium affirmat, eos esse «animantia ærea, seu ætherea acerrimi sensus.» Et de Civit. Dei lib. 11. c. 23, affirmat «Dæmonem pessimum habere corpus æreum.» Et lib. 21. c. 10. scripsit: «Sunt sua quædam etiam Dæmonibus corpora, sicut doctis hominibus visum est, ex isto ære crasso et humido.» Et lib. 15. c. 23. ait «se non audere definire, an Angeli corpore æreo, ita corporati possint etiam hanc pati libidinem, ut quomodo possint, sentientibus fœminis misceantur.» Et in Enarrat. in Psal. 85. ait «corpora beatorum futura post resurrectionem, qualia sunt corpora Angelorum;» et Enarrat. in Psal. 14. 5. ait «corpus Angelicum inferius esse anima.» Et lib. De Divinit. Dæmonum, *passim per totum, maxime c. 23., docet* «Dæmones subtilia habere corpora.»

90. Potest etiam sententia nostra aucthoritatibus Sacræ Scripturæ comprobari, quæ licet ab Expositoribus aliter declarentur, non incongrue tamen ad nostrum intentum possunt aptari. Prima est Psalmi 77., v. 24. et 25., ubi habetur: panem Angelorum manducavit homo, panem cœli dedit eis. *Hic loquitur David de Manna, qua cibatus fuit Populus Israel toto tempore, quo peregrinus fuit in deserto. Quærendum ergo venit, quo sensu Manna dici possit* panis Angelorum. *Scio quidem plerosque Doctores exponere hunc passum in sensu mystico, aientes in Manna figuratam esse* Sacram Eucharistiam, *quæ vocatur* panis Angelorum, *quia Angeli fruuntur visione Dei, qui per concomitantiam in Eucharistia reperitur.*

91. Sed hæc expositio aptissima est quidem, et quam amplectitur Ecclesia in officio Sanctissimi Corporis Christi, *sed in sensu spirituali est. Ego autem quæro sensum litteralem: neque enim in illo Psalmo David loquitur prophetice de futuris, sicut facit in aliis locis, ut proinde facile non sit sensum litteralem habere; sed loquitur historice de præteritis. Ille enim Psalmus, ut patet legenti, est pura anacephalestis, seu compendium omnium beneficiorum, quæ contulit Deus Populo Hebræo ab egressu ipsius de Aegypto, usque ad tempus Davidis, et in eo versu loquitur de Manna Deserti, ut proinde quæratur quomodo, et quo sensu Manna vocetur Panis Angelorum.*

92. Scio alios, Lyran., Euthim., Bellarm., Titelman., Genebrard., in Psal. 77. v. 24. et 25., interpretari Panem Angelorum Panem ab Angelis paratum, seu Angelorum ministerio a Cœlo demissum; Hugonem autem Cardinalem Panem Angelorum exponere: quia ille cibus hoc efficiebat in Judæis, quod in Angelis efficit cibus illorum, pro parte: Angeli enim non incurrunt infirmitatem. Voluerunt enim expositores Hebræi, ut etiam asseverat Josephus, quod Judæi in Deserto vescentes manna, nec senescerent, nec ægrotarent, nec lassarentur; proinde illa esset tanquam panis, quo vescuntur Angeli, qui nec senio, nec ægritudine, nec lassitudine unquam laborant.

93. Istas quidem expositiones recipere æquum est, utpote tantorum Doctorum aucthoritate suffultas. Facessit tamen difficultatem, quod ministerio Angelorum Hebræis non minus parata fuere columna nubis, et ignis, coturnices, et aqua de petra, quam manna; nec tamen ista dicta fuere columna, aqua, aut potus Angelorum. Cur ergo potius vocari deberet manna, quia parata ministerio Angelorum, Panis Angelorum, *quam* Potus Angelorum aqua eorumdem ministerio saxo educta? Insuper in sacra Scriptura panis dum dicitur panis alicujus, *dicitur* panis ejus*qui illo vescitur, non ejus qui illum parat, aut fabricat, et de hoc infinita habemus exempla in sacra Scriptura: ut* Exod. c. 23. v. 25. Benedicam panibus tuis, et aquis; *lib. 2. Reg. c. 12. v. 3.* De pane illius comedens; Tob.*c. 4. v. 17.* Panem tuum cum egenis comede; *et v. 18.* Panem tuum super sepulturam Justi constitue; Ecclesiast. c. 11. v. 1. Mitte panem tuum super transeuntes aquas; Isai. c. 58. v. 7. Frange esurienti panem tuum; Jerem. c. 11. v. 19. Mittamus lignum in panem ejus; Matth. c. 15. v. 26. Non est bonum sumere panem filiorum; Luc. c. 11. v. 3. Panem nostrum quotidianum. *Ex quibus locis patenter habetur, quod panis dicitur ejus, qui eo vescitur, non vero, qui ipsum conficit, affert, aut parat. Commode igitur in loco citato Psalmi accipi potest* Panis Angelorum, *cibus quo vescuntur Angeli non quidem incorporei (isti enim materiali cibo non egent), sed corporei, ista nempe rationalia animalia, de quibus hucusque disseruimus, degentia in ære, et quæ ratione tenuitatis suorum corporum, ac rationalis naturæ, quam maxime ad Angelos immateriales accedunt, ut proinde nuncupentur.*

94. Ducor, quia cum animalia sint, et ideo generabilia et corruptibilia, egent cibo, ut restauretur substantia corporea, quæ per effluvia deperditur; vita enim sentientis non consistit nisi in motu partium corporearum quæ fluunt, ac refluunt, acquiruntur, ac deperduntur, ac iterum reparantur; quæ reparatio fit per substantias spirituosas, materiales tamen, attractas a vivente, tum per æris inspirationem, tum per fermentationem cibi, per quam substantia illius spiritualizatur, ut rationatur doctissimus Ettmullerus, Instit. Medic. Physiolog., *c. 2.*

95. Quia autem eorum corpus tenue est, tenui pariter, et subtili eget alimento. Hinc est quod sicut odoribus aliisque substantiis vaporosis, ac volatilibus suæ naturæ contrariis læduntur ac fugantur, ut constat ex historiis recitatis supra, n° 71. et 72., ita paribus rebus sibi convenientibus delectantur, et aluntur. Porro manna non est aliud, quam halitus aquæ, terræque, solis calore exacte attenuatus et coctus, a frigore secutæ noctis in unum coactus, densatusque, *ut scribit Cornelius; manna dico, quam demissam de cœlo comederunt Hebræi, quæ toto cœlo differt a manna nostrate, quæ in medicinis adhibetur; nam hæc, ut scribit Ettmullerus Schroder,* Dilucid. Physiolog., *c. 1.* de Manna, *fol. m. 154.*, nihil aliud est, quam succus quarumdam arborum tenuis, vel earum transsudatio, quæ nocturno tempore permixta cum rore, matutino tempore superventu caloris solis coagulatur, et inspissatur. *Manna autem Hebræorum diversis orta principiis calore solis non coagulabatur, sed vice versa liquefiebat, ut patet ex Scriptura,* Exod. c. 16. v. 22. Manna ergo Hebræorum utpote constans ex halitibus tenuibus terræ et aquæ, profecto tenuissimæ erat substantiæ, utpote, quæ a sole solvebatur, et disparebat; optime ergo potuit esse talium animalium cibus, ita ut diceretur a David Panis Angelorum.

96. Alia auctoritas habetur in Evangelio Joannis, in quo, Joannes, *c. 10. v. 16., ita dicitur:* Alias oves habeo, quæ non sunt ex hoc ovili, et illas oportet me adducere, et vocem meam audient, et fiet unum ovile, et unus Pastor. Si quæramus quænam sint oves, quæ non sunt ex hoc ovili, et qualenam sit ovile de quo loquitur Christus Dominus, respondent communiter Expositores unum ovile Christi esse Ecclesiam, ad quam perducendi erant per prædicationem Evangelii Gentiles, qui erant oves alterius ovilis, ab ovili Hebræorum: opinantur enim Synagogam esse Christi ovile, quia dicebat David, Psal. 94. v. 9: Nos populus ejus et oves pascuæ ejus; *et quia Messias promissus fuerat Abraham et David oriturus ex eorum semine, et a populo Hebræo expectatus, et a Prophetis qui Hebræi erant vaticinatus, et ejus adventus, conversatio, passio, mors et resurrectio in sacrificiis, cultu, et ceremoniis Hebræorum legis erant præfigurata.*

97. Sed salva semper Sanctorum Patrum, ac aliorum Doctorum reverentia, non videtur talis expositio ad plenum satisfacere. Habemus enim quod de fide est a principio mundi Ecclesiam Fidelium extitisse unam, usque ad finem sæculi duraturam. Cujus Ecclesiæ caput est mediator Dei et hominum Christus Jesus, cujus contemplatione creata sunt universa, et omnia per ipsum facta. Fides enim unius Dei Trini (quamvis non ita explicite), et Verbi Incarnatio revelata fuit primo homini, et ab ipso edocti ejus filii, et ab iis descendentes. Hinc est quod quamvis plerique homines ad idolatriam deflexerint, ac veram fidem deseruerint, multi tamen veram fidem a patribus sibi traditam retinuerunt, et legem naturæ servantes

in vera Ecclesia Fidelium permanserunt, ut observat Cardinalis Toletus in Job, *c.*
10. v. 16., et apparet in Job, *qui inter Gentiles Idololatras sanctus fuit. Quamvis*
autem Deus populo Hebræo speciales favores contulerit, peculiaremque legem, ac
ceremonias illi præscripserit, ac a Gentilibus segregaverit, non tamen ad eam legem
Gentes tenebantur, nec fideles Hebræi aliam Ecclesiam constituebant ab Ecclesia
Gentilium, qui fidem unius Dei et Messiæ venturi profitebantur.

98. Hinc est, quod etiam ex Gentilibus fuere, qui Christi adventum, et alia Chris-
tianæ fidei dogmata prophetarunt, ut patet de Balaam, Mercurio Trismegisto, Hy-
daspe, *ac* Sibyllis de quibus loquitur Lactantius, lib. 1. c. 6., ut scribit Cardinalis
Baronius in Apparatu Annal. n° 18. Et quod Messias erat a Gentilibus expectatus
habet Isaias in pluribus locis, et luculentum testimonium de hoc est prophetia
Patriarchæ Jacob de Messia, quæ sic ait, Gen. c. 49. v. 10: Non auferetur sceptrum
de Juda, et dux de femore ejus, donec veniat qui mittendus est, et ipse erit expec-
tatio Gentium. *Item Prophetia Aggæi, c. 2. v. 8:* Movebo omnes Gentes, et veniet
desideratus cunctis gentibus, *quem locum explicans Cornelius a Lap. in* Aggæ. c.
2. v. 8. § Denique gentes, *ait:* Gentes ante Christum credentes in Deum lege
naturæ, æque ac Judæi expectabant ac desiderabant Christum. *Pariter Christus*
ita se prodidit, et manifestavit Gentibus, sicut Judæis: si enim in ipsius nativitate
per Angelum ejus notitia data fuit Pastoribus, per stellam miraculosam ad sui
adorationem vocavit Magos, qui cum essent Gentiles fuerunt primitiæ Gentium
in Christo agnoscendo, et adorando, ut ait S. Fulgentius, Sermon. 6. de Epiph.,
sicut Pastores fuerunt primitiæ Judæorum. Itidem manifestatio adventus Christi
per prædicationem (non quidem Apostolorum) prius facta est Gentilibus, quam
Judæis: siquidem ut scribit Ven. Mater Soror Maria de Agreda, in Vita J. C. et B.
M. V., *p. 1. l. 4. c. 26. n. 664:* Quando B. M. Virgo cum S. Joseph portavit Puerum
Jesum in Aegyptum, fugiendo Herodis persecutionem, mansit ibi per septen-
nium: quo tempore ipsa Beatissima Virgo prædicavit Aegyptiis veri Dei fidem,
et Filii Dei in carne humana adventum. *Ulterius in Christi nativitate multa fuere*
prodigia non solum in Judæa, sed in Aegypto, ubi corruerunt idola, ac oracula
conticuere; Romæ ubi fons olei scaturiit; visus globus aurei coloris de cælo in ter-
ram descendere; apparuere tres soles; ac contra naturam circulus variegatus ad
modum Iridis solis discum circumscripsit; in Græcia, ubi oraculum Delphicum
obmutuit, et interrogatus Apollo ab Augusto ipsi sacrificante in proprio palatio,
ubi eidem aram extruxerat, de causa silentii sui, respondit, ut referunt Nicephorus,
l. 1. c. 17., Suidas, verbo Augustus, *et Cedrenus,*Compend. Histor.:

Me puer Hebræus, Divos Deus ipse gubernans,
Cedere sede jubet, tristemque redire sub orcum;
Aris ergo dehinc tacitis abscedito nostris.
Et multa alia acciderunt prodigia, quibus prænuntiabatur Gentilibus Filii Dei adventus, quæ ex variis Aucthoribus recitat Baronius, Apparat. Annal. Eccles. nᵒ 24. et seq., et Cornelius in Aggæ. c. 2. v. 8.

99. Ex istis patet, quod etiam Gentiles pertinebant ad ovile Christi idem, ad quod spectabant Judæi, puta ad Ecclesiam eamdem fidelem; igitur non potest recte dici, quod illa verba Christi: Alias oves habeo, quæ non sunt ex hoc ovili, *accipienda sint de Gentilibus, qui communem cum Hebræis habuerunt de Deo fidem, de Messia spem, prophetiam, expectationem, et signa, et prædicationem.*

100. Dico igitur quod nomine aliarum ovium commode possunt intelligi Creaturæ istæ rationales, sive animalia de quibus hucusque disseruimus. Cum enim, ut diximus, capaces sint beatitudinis, et damnationis, et Christus Jesus sit mediator Dei, et hominum, immo totius rationalis Creaturæ (creaturæ enim rationales, quæ beatitudinem consequuntur, hanc obtinent intuitu meritorum Christi per ab eo sibi collatam gratiam, sine qua nequit beatitudo obtineri), debuit omnis rationalis creatura *de eo venturo spem habere, sicut de uno Deo fidem, et de ipsius in carne nativitate, et de præceptis legis gratiæ manifestationem. Istæ igitur erant oves, quæ non erant* ex hoc ovili humano, *et quas adducere Christum oportebat, et quæ ejus vocem nempe notitiam de ipsius adventu, et de evangelica doctrina, quantum per se, tum per Apostolos Christus erat manifestaturus audire debebant, et ex iis, ac hominibus in cœlo beatificatis fieri* unum ovile, et unus Pastor.

101. Huic expositioni quam incongruam non puto, vim addit id quod supra nᵒ 77. ex D. Hieronymo retulimus de homunculo illo qui rogavit D. Antonium, ut communem Deum, quem in carne humana esse passum cognoverat, pro se et suis deprecaretur. *Innuitur enim ex his, quod illi notitiam habuerunt de adventu, et morte Christi, quem tamquam Deum optabant sibi propitium, ut proinde ad hoc intercessionem D. Antonii expostularent.*

102. Facit ad idem id, quod ex Eusebio de Præparat. Evang. l. 5. c. 9., et Plutarcho l. de Defectu Oracul., *refert Cardinalis Baronius* Appar. Annal. nᵒ 129., et recenset inter prodigia, quæ tempore mortis Christi evenere. Recitat igitur ex citatis

Aucthoribus quod Tiberii Imperatoris, sub quo passus est Christus, tempore, navigantibus nonnullis a Græcia in Italiam, circa Insulas Echinades, cessatis ventis, noctu navigium appulit prope terram. Audita fuit ab omnibus vox magna quæ vocavit Tramnum. Erat is Nauclerus navigii, quo respondente Adsum, *replicavit vox:* Quando perveneris prope quandam paludem, annunciabis Magnum Pana mortuum esse: *quod cum Tramnus fecisset, auditi sunt repente multorum, imo multitudinis prope infinitæ gemitus, et ululatus. Profecto isti fuerunt Dæmones, seu Angeli corporei, seu animalia rationalia prope paludem degentia, utpote aquea, quæ audita morte Christi, qui nomine magni Pan efferebatur, in lacrymas, et lamenta effusa sunt; prout etiam Hebræi nonnulli visa Christi morte percutientes pectora sua revertebantur* (Luc. c. 23. v. 48.). Ex hucusque igitur deductis patet, quod dantur hujusmodi Dæmones, succubi et incubi, constantes sensu, et ipsius passionibus obnoxii, ut probatum est; qui generantur, corrumpuntur, et capaces sunt beatitudinis, et damnationis, et ratione corporis subtilioris, nobiliores homine sunt, et qui si cum hominibus, maribus aut fœminis, carnaliter commiscentur, peccant, et eo peccato, quo peccat homo jungendo se cum bruto, quod est homine ignobilius; proinde non raro hi Dæmones consuetudinem habentes cum homine, equabus aut plurimum post longam habitam communicationem eas interficiunt. Causa porro hujus est, quod si inter tales datur peccatum, cum sint in via, dari etiam debet pœnitentia; sicut ergo homini peccanti consuetudinaliter cum bruto, ad tollendam occasionem recidivandi, Confessarius injungit, ut brutum tollat de medio, ita tali Dæmoni consuetudinario in peccato, et tandem pœnitenti accidit, ut animal cum quo peccavit, sive homo, sive brutum fuerit, occidat; nec enim tali Dæmoni mors data homini peccatum erit, sicut mors data bruto non imputatur tamquam peccatum homini: ratione enim essentialis differentiæ inter Dæmonem hujusmodi, et hominem, idem erit homo Dæmoni, quod est homini brutum.

103. Scio multos, et forte plerosque, qui hæc legerint, dicturos de me, quod Epicurei, et Stoici Philosophi nonnulli dixerunt de Divo Paulo, Actor.c. 17. v. 18.: Novorum Dæmoniorum videtur annunciator, *et datam doctrinam exsibillabunt. Sed isti tenebuntur solvere argumenta supra posita, et dicere quinam sint Dæmones isti Incubi vulgo* Folletti, *qui exorcismos, res sacras, et Christi Crucem non pavent, ac alios effectus istorum, ac phænomena salvare, quæ nos ex data doctrina ostendimus.*

104. Solvitur ergo ex his, quæ hucusque deducta sunt, quæstio, quam propo-

suimus supra n° 30. et n° 34.: resolutive innuimus; quomodo mulier potest ingravidari a Dæmone Incubo. Non enim hoc præstare potest ex semine sumpto ab homine, ut fert communis opinio, quam confutavimus n° 31 et 32: sequitur ergo, quod ipsa imprægnatur a semine Incubi, cum enim animal sit, et generet, proprio pollet semine: et hoc modo optime salvatur generatio Gigantum secuta ex commixtione Filiorum Dei cum Filiabus hominum; nati siquidem sunt ex tali concubitu Gigantes, qui licet homini essent similes, corpore tamen erant majores: et quamvis a Dæmonibus geniti, viribus proinde pollerent, non tamen Dæmonum vires et potentiam æquabant, ut sequitur in mulis, hinnis et burdonibus, qui medii *quodammodo sunt inter eas species animalium, a quibus promiscue generantur, et superant quidem imperfectiorem, non attingunt autem perfectiorem speciem generantium: mulus enim superat asinum, sed non æquat perfectionem equæ, a quibus generatur.*

105. *Confirmat autem hanc sententiam consideratio, quod animalia genita ex commixtione diversarum specierum non generant; sed sunt sterilia, ut patet in mulis. Gigantes autem non leguntur Gigantes generasse, sed natos a Filiis Dei, puta Incubis, et filiabus hominum: cum enim concepti fuerint ex semine Dæmoniaco mixto cum humano, non potuerunt, tamquam mediæ speciei inter Dæmonem et hominem, generare.*

106. *Dicetur fortasse contra hoc, non posse, ex semine Dæmonum, quod pro sui natura oportet esse tenuissimum, fieri mixturam cum semine humano, quod crassum est; unde nec generatio sequi possit.*

107. *Respondeo quod, ut dictum fuit supra n° 32*: virtus generandi consistit in spiritu, qui simul cum materia spumosa et viscida deciditur a generante; sequitur ex hoc, quod semen Dæmonis quantumvis tenuissimum, quia tamen materiale, optime potest commisceri cum spiritu materiali seminis humani, ac fieri generatio.

108. *Replicabitur adhuc contra conclusionem, quod si vere fuisset Gigantum generatio ex semine Incuborum et Mulierum, nunc quoque Gigantes nascerentur, non desunt enim mulieres coeuntes cum Incubis, ut patet ex gestis SS. Bernardi et Petri de Alcantara, et aliarum historiarum, quæ passim ab Auctoribus recitantur.*

109. Respondeo, quod prout ex Guaccio dictum fuit supra n°81: alii sunt hujus-modi Dæmones terrei, alii aquei, ærei alii, et alii ignei, qui respective in propriis eorum elementis habitant. Videmus autem animalia eo majora esse, quo majus est elementum in quo degunt, ut patet in piscibus, inter quos licet multi sint minuti, ut etiam sunt plura animalia terrestria minutissima, et tamen quia elementum aquæ majus est elemento terræ (utpote continens majus semper est contento), ideo pisces a tota specie superant in magnitudine molis animalia terrestria, ut patet in balenis, orcynis, pistis seu pistricibus, thynnis, ac aliis piscibus cetaceis, seu viviparis, qui quodvis animal terrestre longe superant. Porro cum Dæmones hujusmodi animalia sint, ut hucusque probatum est, eo erunt majores in mag-nitudine quo elementum majus pro sui natura inhabitabunt. Et cum ær excedat aquam, et ignis ære major sit, sequitur, quod Dæmones ætherei, ac ignei longe superabunt terrestres et aqueos, tum in mole corporis, tum in virtute. Nec contra hoc facit instantia de avibus, qui licet incolant ærem, qui major est aqua, ta-men corpore minores sunt a tota specie piscibus et quadrupedibus, quia aves licet per ærem volatu spatientur, revera tamen pertinent ad elementum terræ, in qua quiescunt; aliter enim pisces nonnulli qui volant, ut hirundo marina, et alii, dici deberent animalia ærea, quod falsum est.

110. Advertendum autem, quod post diluvium ær iste terraqueo globo citissimus magis incrassatus est ex humiditate aquarum, quam fuerit ante diluvium, et hinc forte est, quod ex tali humido, quod est principium corruptionis, fiat, quod ho-mines non ætatem ita producant, ut faciebant ante diluvium. Ex ista autem æris crassitie fit, quod Dæmones ætherei, ac ignei, cæteris corpulentiores, nequeunt diutius manere in hoc ære crasso, et si descendunt aliquando hoc fit violenter, et eo modo quo urinatores ad ima maris descendunt.

111. Ante diluvium autem, cum adhuc ær non ita crassus erat, veniebant Dæ-mones, et cum mulieribus miscebantur, et gigantes procreabant, qui magnitudi-nem corpoream Dæmonum generantium æmulabantur. Nunc vero ita non est: Dæmones enim Incubi, qui fœminas incessunt, sunt aquei quorum corporis moles magna non est: et proinde in forma homuncionum apparent, et quia aquei etiam salacissimi sunt; luxuria enim in humido est: ut proinde Venerem e mari natam Poetæ finxerint, quod Mythologi explicant de libidine, quæ oritur ab humiditate. Cum ergo Dæmones, qui corpore parvi sunt, his temporibus mulieres impræg-nent, non gigantes, sed staturæ ordinariæ filii nascuntur. Sciendum porro quod si miscentur corporaliter cum mulieribus Dæmones in sua ipsorum corpulentia naturali, nulla facta immutatione aut artificio, mulieres illos non vident, nisi tanquam umbram pæne incertam, ac quasi insensibilem, ut patet in muliere illa, de qua diximus supra n° 28., quæ osculabatur ab incubo, cujus tactus vix ab ea sentiebatur. Quando vero volunt se visibiles amasiis reddere, atque ipsis delectationem in congressu carnali afferre, sibi indumentum visibile assumunt, et corpus crassum reddunt. Qua vero hoc arte fiat, ipsi norunt. Nobis curta nostra Philosophia hoc non pandit. Unum scire possumus, et est, quod tale indumentum seu corpus ex solo ære concreto constare nequiret, hoc enim esse deberet per condensationem, et proinde per frigus; unde oporteret, quod corpus illud ad tactum esset veluti glacies, et ita in coitu mulieres non delectaret, sed torqueret, cum tamen contrarium eveniat.

112. Visa igitur differentia Dæmonum spiritualium, qui cum sagis coeunt, et Incuborum, qui cum fœminis minime sagis rem habent, perpendenda est gravitas hujus criminis in utroque casu.

113. In coitu Sagarum cum Dæmonibus, eo quia non fit nisi cum apostasia a Fide, et Diaboli cultu, et tot aliis impietatibus quas recensuimus supra a n° 12. ad 24., est maximum quorumque peccatorum, quæ ab hominibus fieri possunt: et ratione tantæ enormitatis contra Religionem, quæ præsupponitur coitu cum Diabolo, profecto Dæmonialitas maximum est criminum carnalium. Sed spectato delicto carnis ut sic, et ut abstracto a peccatis contra Religionem, Dæmonialitas redigenda est ad simplicem pollutionem. Ratio, et quidem convincentissima, est quia Diabolus, qui rem habet cum sagis, purus spiritus est, et est in termino ac damnatus ut dictum supra fuit; proinde si cum sagis coit, hoc facit in corpore assumpto, aut a se formato, ut sentiunt communiter Theologi. Porro corpus illud quamvis moveatur, non tamen vivens est; sequitur ergo quod coiens cum tali corpore, sive mas sive fœmina fuerit, idem delictum committit, ac si cum corpore inanimato, aut cadavere coiret, quod esset simplex mollities, ut alias demonstravimus. Verum est, quod, ut observavit etiam Cajetanus, talis coitus effective potest habere deformitates aliorum criminum juxta corpus a Diabolo assumptum, et vas: si enim assumeret corpus virginis consanguineæ, aut sacræ, effective esset tale crimen incestus aut sacrilegium, et si in figura bruti coiret, aut in vase præpostero, evaderet bestialitas, aut Sodomia.

114. In coitu autem cum Incubo, in quo nulla habetur qualitas, vel minima, criminis contra Religionem, difficile est rationem invenire, per quam tale delictum Bestialitate et Sodomia gravior esset. Siquidem gravitas Bestialitatis præ Sodomia, prout supra diximus, consistit in hoc, quod homo vilificat dignitatem suæ speciei jungendose cum bruto, quod est speciei longe inferioris sua. In coitu autem cum Incubo diversa est ratio: nam Incubus ratione spiritus rationalis, ac immortalis, æqualis est homini; ratione vero corporis nobilioris, nempe subtilioris, est perfectior, et dignior homine; et hoc modo homo jungens se Incubo non vilificat, immo dignificat suam naturam, et ita, juxta hanc considerationem, Dæmonialitas nequit esse gravior Bestialitate.

115. Tamen gravior communiter censetur, et ratio, meo videri, potest esse: quia peccatum contra Religionem est, quævis communicatio cum Diabolo, sive ex pacto, sive non; puta habendo cum eo consuetudinem aut familiaritatem, seu ab eo petendo auxilium consilium, favorem, aut ab ipso quærendo revelationem futurorum, relationem præteritorum, absentium, aut alias occultorum. Hujusmodi autem homines, seu mulieres, concumbendo cum Incubis, quos nesciunt animalia esse, sed putant esse diabolos, contra conscientiam erroneam delinquunt; et hoc modo ex conscientia erronea ita peccant cum Incubis se jungendo, ac si cum diabolis coirent: unde et gravitatem ejusdem criminis incurrunt.

FINIS

Appendix

THE MANUSCRIPT OF *Demoniality* breaks oft with the conclusion just given. In a purely philosophical and theoretical acception, the work is complete: for it was enough that the author should define, in general terms, the grievousness of the crime,- without concerning himself with the proceedings which were to make out the proof, nor with the penalty to be inflicted. Both those questions, on the contrary, had, as a matter of course, a place assigned to them in the great work *De Delictis et Pœnis,* which is a veritable *Code for the Inquisitor*; and Father Sinistrari of Ameno could not fail to treat them there with all the care and conscientiousness he has so amply shown in the foregoing pages. The reader will be happy to find here that practical conclusion to *Demoniality*.

(Note by Lisieux)

Proof of Demoniality

1. *Distinctions to be made in the proof of the crime of Demoniality.*
2. *Signs proving the intercourse of a Witch with the Devil.*
3. *The confession of the Sorcerer himself is requisite for a full eviction.*
4. *Tale of a Nun who had an intimacy with an Incubus.*
5. *If the indictment is supported by the recitals of eye-witnesses, torture may be resorted to.*

1. As regards the proof of that crime, a distinction must be made of the kind of Demoniality, to wit: whether it is that which is practiced by Witches or Wizards with the Devil, or that which other persons perpetrate with Incubi.

2. In the first case, the compact entered into with the Devil being proved, the evidence of Demoniality follows as a necessary consequence; for,the purpose, both of Witches and Wizards, in the nightly revels that take place after feasting and dancing, is none other but that infamous intercourse; otherwise there can be no witness of that crime, since the Devil, visible to the Witch, escapes the sight of others. Sometimes, it is true, women have been seen in the woods, in the fields, in the groves, lying on their backs, *ad umbilicum tenus nudata, et juxta dispositionem actus venerei*, their legs *divaricatis et adductis, dunes agitare*, as is written by Guaccius, *book I, chap.*

12, v. Sciendum est scepius, fol. 65. In such a case there would be a very strong suspicion of such a crime, if supported by other signs; and I am inclined to believe that such action, sufficiently proved by witnesses, would justify the Judge in resorting to torture in order to ascertain the truth; especially if, shortly after that action, a sort of black smoke had been seen to issue from the woman, and she had been noticed to rise, as is also written by Guaccius; for it might be inferred that that smoke or shadow had been the Devil himself, *concumbens cum foemina*. Likewise if, as has more than once happened, according to the same author, a woman had been seen concumbere cum homine, who, the action over, suddenly disappeared.

3. Moreover, in order to prove conclusively that a person is a Wizard or a Witch, the own confession of such person is requisite: for there can be no witnesses to the fact, unless perhaps other Sorcerers giving evidence at the trial against their accomplices; from their being confederates in the crime, their statement is not conclusive and does not justify the recourse to torture, should not other indications be forthcoming, such as the seal of the Devil stamped on their body, as aforesaid, Number 23, or the finding in their dwelling, after a search, of signs and instruments of the diabolic art: for instance, bones and, especially, a skull, hair artfully plaited, intricate knots of feathers, wings, feet or bones of bats, toads or serpents, unfamiliar seeds, wax figures, vessels filled with unknown powder, oil or ointments, etc., as are usually detected by Judges who, upon a charge being brought against Sorcerers, proceed to their apprehension and the search of their houses.

4. The proof of intimacy with an Incubus offers the same difficulty; for, no less than other Demons, the Incubus is, at will, invisible to all but his mistress. Yet, it has not seldom happened that Incubi have allowed themselves to be surprised in the act of carnal intercourse with women, now in one shape, how in another. In a Monastery (I mention neither its name nor that of the town where it lies, so as not to recall to memory a past scandal), there was a Nun, who, about trifles, as is usual with women and especially with nuns, had quarrelled with one of her mates who occupied a cell adjoining to hers. Quick at observing all the doings of her enemy, this neighbour noticed, several days in succession, that instead of walking with her companions in the garden after dinner she retired to her cell, where she locked herself in. Anxious to know what she could be doing there all that time, the inquisitive Nun betook herself also to her cell. Soon she heard a sound, as of two voices conversing in subdued tones, which she could easily do, since the two cells were divided but by a slight partition), therf a peculiar friction, the cracking of a bed, groans and sighs, quasi duorum concumbentium; her curiositywas raised to the highest pitch, and she redoubled her attention in order to ascertain who was in the cell. But having, three times running, seen no other nun come out but her rival, she suspected that a man had been secretly introduced and was kept hidden there. She went and reported the thing to the Abbess, who, after holding counsel with discreet persons, resolved upon hearing the sounds and observing the indications that had been denounced her, so as to avoid any precipitate or inconsiderate act. In consequence, the Abbess and her confidents repaired to the cell of the spy, and heard the voices and

other noises that had been described. An inquiry was set on foot to make sure whether any of the Nuns could be shut in with the other one; and the result being in the negative, the Abbess and her attendants went to the door of the closed cell, and knocked repeatedly, but to no purpose: the Nun neither answered, nor opened. The Abbess threatened to have the door broken in, and even ordered a convert to force it with a crow-bar. The Nun then opened her door: a search was made and no one found. Being asked with whom she had been talking, and the why and wherefore of the bed cracking, of the sighs, etc., she denied every thing. But, matters going on just the same as before, the rival Nun, become more attentive and more inquisitive than ever, contrived to bore a hole through the partition, so as to be able to see what was going on inside the cell; and what should she see but an elegant youth lying with the Nun, and the sight of whom she took care to let the others enjoy by the same means. The charge was soon brought before the bishop: the guilty Nun endeavoured still to deny all; but, threatened with the torture, she. confessed having had an intimacy with an Incubus.

5. When, therefore, indications are forthcoming, such as those recited above, a charge might be brought after a searching inquiry; yet, without the confession of the accused, the offence should not be regarded as fully proved, even if the intercourse were testified by eye-witnesses; for it sometimes happens that, in order to undo an innocent female, the Devil feigns such intercourse by means of some delusion. In those cases, the Ecclesiastical Judge must consequently trust but his own eyes.

Probatio Dæmonialitatis
SUMMARIUM

1. De probatione criminis Dæmonialitatis, distinguendum est.
2. Indicia probantia coitum Sagæ cum Diabolo.
3. Requiritur confessio ipsius malefici ad plenam probationem.
4. Historia de Moniali habente consuetudinem cum Incubo.
5. Si adsint indicia visa in recitata historia, potest ad torturam deveniri.

1. Quantum ad probationem hujus criminis attinet, distinguendum est de Dæmonialitate, puta, vel ejus, quæ a Sagis, seu Maleficis fit cum Diabolis; sive de ea, quæ ab aliis fit cum Incubis.

2. Quoad primam, probato crimine pacti facti cum Diabolo, probata remanet *Dæmonialitas ex consequentia necessaria; nam scopus tum Sagarum, tum Maleficorum in ludis nocturnis, ultra convivia, et choreas, est hujusmodi infamis congressus: aliter, illius criminis nullus potest esse testis, quia Diabolus, qui Sagæ visibilis est, aliorum oculos effugit. Verum est, quod aliquoties visæ sunt mulieres in sylvis, agris, et nemoribus, supinæ jacentes, ad umbilicum tenus denudatæ, et juxta dispositionem actus venerei, divaricatis, et adductis cruribus, clunes agitare, prout scribit Guacc., lib. p. cap. 12, v. Sciendum est sæpius, fol. 65. Tali casu emergeret suspicio vehemens talis criminis, dummodo esset aliunde adminiculata, et crederem talem actum per testes sufficienter probatum, sufficere Judici ad indagandam tormentis veritatem; et hoc maxime, si post aliqualem moram in illo actu, visus fuisset a muliere elevari quasi fumus niger, et tunc mulierem surgere, prout ibidem scribit Guaccius; talis enim fumus, aut umbra, Dæmonem fuisse concumbentem cum fœmina inferre potest. Sicut etiam, si mulier visa fuisset concumbere cum homine, qui post actum de repente evanuit, ut non semel accidisse idem auctor ibidem narrat.*

3. Cæterum, ad probandum concludenter aliquem esse Maleficum, seu Maleficam, requiritur propria Confessio; nullus enim haberi potest de hoc testis, nisi forte sint alii Malefici, qui in judicio deponunt de complicibus; sed quia socii criminis sunt, eorum dictum non concludit, nec etiam ad torturam sufficit, nisi alia exstent indicia, puta, sigillum Diaboli impressum in eorum corpore, prout

diximus supra num. 23.; et in eorum domibus, facta perquisitione, inveniantur signa, ac instrumenta artis diabolicæ, ut ossa mortuorum, præsertim calvariam; crines artificiose contextos; nodos plumarum intricatos; alas, aut pedes, aut ossicula vespertilionum, aut bufonum, aut serpentium; ignotas seminum species; figuras cereas; vasculos plenos incognito pulvere, aut oleo, aut unguentis minime notis, etc., ut ordinarie contingit reperiri a Judicibus, qui, accepta accusatione de hujusmodi Sagis, ad capturam, et domus visitationem deveniunt, ut scribit Delbene, de Off. S. Inquis., *Par. 2. Dub. 206. num. 7.*

4. Quantum vero ad probationem congressus cum Incubo, par est difficultas; non minus enim Incubus, ac alii Diaboli effugiunt, quando volunt, visum aliorum, ut videri se faciunt a sola amasia. Tamen non raro accidit, quod etiam visi sint Incubi modo sub una, modo sub alia specie in actu carnali cum mulieribus.

In quodam Monasterio (nomen ejus et urbis taceo, ne veterem ignominiam memoriæ refricem) quædam fuit Monialis, quæ cum alia Moniali, quæ cellam habebat suæ contiguam, simultatem ex levibus causis, ut assolet inter Mulieres, maxime Religiosas, habebat. Hæc sagax in observando quascunque actiones Monialis sibi adversæ, per plures dies vidit, quod ista in diebus æstivis, statim a prandio non spatiabatur per viridarium cum aliis, sed ab iis sequestra, se retrahebat in cellam, quam sera obserabat. Observatrix igitur æmula curiositate investigans, quid tali tempore illa facere posset, etiam ipsa in propriam cellam se recipiebat; cœpit autem audire submissam quasi duorum insimul colloquentium vocem (quod facile erat, nam cella parvo simplicis, scilicet lateris unius, disterminio dividebatur), mox sonitum poppysmatum,[1] *concussionis lecti, gannitus, ac anhelitus, quasi duorum concumbentium; unde aucta in æmula curiositate, accuratius stetit in observatione, ut sciret, quinam in illa cella essent. Postquam autem per tres vices vidit, nullam aliam Monialem egressam e cella illa, præter æmulam, dominam cellæ, suspicata est, Monialem in camera absconditum aliquem virum, clanculum introductum retinere; unde et rem detulit ad Abbatissam, quæ consilio habita cum Discretis, voluit audire sonitus, et observare indicia relata ab accusatrice, ne præcipitanter, et inconsiderate ageret. Abbatissa igitur cum Discretis se receperunt in Cellam observatricis, et audierunt strepitus, et voces, quas accusatrix detulerat. Facta igitur inquisitione, an ulla Monialium potuisset secum in illa Cella clausa esse, et reperto, quod non; Abbatissa cum Discretis fuit ad ostium Cellæ clausæ, et pulsato frustra pluries ostio, cum Monialis nec respondere, nec aperire vellet; Abbatissa minata est, se velle ostium prosterni facere, et vecte aggredi opus fecit a quadam conversa. Tunc aperuit ostium Monialis, et facta perquisitione, nullus inventus est in camera. Interrogata Monialis cum quonam loqueretur, et de causa concussionis lecti, anhelituum, etc., omnia negavit.*

Cum vero res perseveraret, accuratior, ac curiosior reddita Monialis æmula perforavit tabulas lacunaris, ut posset Cellam introspicere; et vidit elegantem quemdam juvenem cum Moniali concumbentem, quem etiam eodem modo ab aliis Monialibus videndum curavit. Delata mox accusatione ad Episcopum, ipsaque Moniali omnia negante, tandem metu tormentorum comminatorum adacta, confessa est, se cum Incubo consuetudinem habuisse.

5. Quando igitur adessent talia indicia, sicut in recitata historia intervenerunt, posset utique in rigoroso examine Rea constitui; sine tamen ejus confessione, non censendum est delictum plene probatum, quantumvis a testibus visus fuisset congressus; siquidem aliquando accidit, quod Diabolus ut infamiam alicui innocenti pararet, præstigiose talem concubitum repræsentaverit. Unde in his casibus debet Judex Ecclesiasticus esse perfecte oculatus.

NOTE:

1. *Poppysmatum.* — That word being but little used, it may be useful to record here the definition given of it by the Glossarium eroticum linguae latince (auctore P. P., Paris, 1826): Poppysma. — Oris pressi sonus, similis illi quo permulcentur equi et canes. Obscene vero de susurro cunni labiorum, quum frictu madescunt.

Father Sinistrari, well versed in classical literature, had turned to account the following epigram of Martial (book VII, 18):

IN GALLAM

Quum tibi sit facies, de qua nec foemina possit
Dicere, quum corpus nulla litura notet;
Cur te tarn rarus cupiat, repetatque fututor,
Miraris? Vitium est non leve, Galla, tibi.
Accessi quoties ad opus, mixtisque movemur
Inguinibus, cunnus non tacet, ipsa taces.
Di facerent, ut tu loquereris, et ipse taceret!
Offender cunni garrulitate tui.
Pedere te mallem: namque hoc nec inutile dicit
Symmachus, et risum res movet ista simul.
Quis ridere potest fatui poppysmata cunni?
Quum sonat hic, cui non mentula mensque cadit
Dic aliquid saltem, clamosoque obstrepe cunno:
Et si adeo muta es, disce vel inde loqui.
(Editorial Note.)

Penalties

As regards the penalties applicable to Demoniality, there is no law that I know of, either civil or canonical, wich inflicts a punishment for a crime of that kind. Since, however, such a crime implies a compact and fellowship with the Demon, and apostasy of the faith, not to speak of the malefices and other almost numberless outrages perpetrated by Sorcerers, as a rule it is punished, out of Italy, by the gallows and the stake. But, in Italy, it is but very seldom that offenders of that kind are delivered up by the Inquisitors to the secular power.

Pœnæ

Quantum ad pœnas Dæmonialitatis, nulla lex Civilis, aut Canonica, quam legerim, reperitur, quæ pœnam sanciat contra crimen hujusmodi. Tamen, quia crimen hoc supponit pactum, ac societatem cum Dæmone, ac apostasiam a fide, ultra veneficia, atque alia infinita propemodum damna, quæ a Maleficis inferuntur, regulariter extra Italiam, suspendio, et incendio punitur. In Italia autem, rarissime traduntur hujusmodi Malefici ab Inquisitoribus Curiæ sæculari.

Biographical Notice

FATHER LUDOVICO MARIA Sinistrari, of the Order of Reformed Minors of the strict Observance of St. Francis, was born in Ameno, a small town of the district of St. Julius, in the diocese of Novara, on the 26th of February 1622. He received a liberal education and went through a course of humanities in Pavia, where, in the year 1647, he entered the Order of Franciscans. Devoting himself henceforward to tuition, he was first a professor of Philosophy; he then, during fifteen successive years, taught Theology in the same town, amidst a numerous concourse of students attracted from all parts of Europe by his high repute. His sermons preached in the principal cities of Italy, at the same time as they caused his eloquence to be admired, were productive of the most happy results for piety. Equally endeared to the World and to Religion, he had been favoured by nature with the most brilliant gifts: square frame, high stature, open countenance, broad forehead, sparkling eyes, high-coloured complexion, pleasant conversation replete with sallies of wit; more valuable still, he was in possession of the gifts of grace, through which he was enabled to sustain, with unconquerable resignation, the assaults of an arthritical disease he was subject to; he was, moreover, remarkable for his meekness, candour and absolute submission to the rules of his Order. A man of all sciences, he had learnt foreign languages without any master, and often, in the general Meetings of his Order, held in Rome, he supported, in public, theses de omni scibili. He, however, addicted himself more particularly to the study of Civil and Canon laws. In Rome he filled the appointment of Consulter to the supreme Tribunal of the Holy-Inquisition; was some time Vicar general of the Archbishop of Avignon, and then Theologian attached to the Archbishop of Milan. In the year 1688, charged by the general Meeting of Franciscans with the compilation of the statutes of the Order, he performed this task in his treatise entitled Practica criminalis Minorum illustrata. He died in the year of our Lord 1701, on the 6th of March, at the age of seventy-nine. [1]

NOTE:
1. This notice is an abstract from: The complete works of P. Sinistrari (Rome, Giannini, 1753-1754,3 vol. in-folio) include the following books: Practica criminalis Minorum illustrata, - Formularium criminate, — De incorrigibilium expulsione ab Ordinibus Regularibus, — De Delictis et Pœnis, to which should be added the present work: De Demonialitate, published for the first time in the year 1875.

Letter

LETTER OF THE
REV. FATHER PROVINCIAL OF CAPUCHINS
FOR THE PROVINCE OF P...

P..., Friday (8 October 1875).

Pax
Monsieur Isidore Liseux,
Paris,

I have gone through the work you sent me yesterday, and have,
indeed, been satisfied with the edition; the time has not yet arrived
for me to give my opinion on' the value of the work itself Here you
would have met with no other works of the Rev. Father Sinistrari
of Ameno than his book: Practica criminalis Minorum; De Delictis
et Pœnis *is to be found, I believe, in another of our convents; but*
you would have been given a most welcome reception. I believe
that Des Grieux can hardly have resided in the present St-Sulpice,
which dates but from the year 1816.

I noticed on page 132-133 a rather serious translation error: you
change Chartreuse du Tessin *into* Carthusia Ticinensis *when it is*
about the famous Chartreuse de Pavia, well known to all travellers in
Italy. There are also, as far as a superficial glance has enabled me to
realize, some other errors; But, on the whole, the work is good, and

you may accept of the congratulations of your very little servant,

Fr. A...

m. p.

Convent of Capuchins, rue ....

Lettre

du
R. P. PROVINCIAL DES CAPUCINS
POUR LA PROVINCE DE P....

P..., vendredi [8 octobre 1875]
†

Pax
Monsieur Isidore Liseux,
5, rue Scribe, Paris.

J'ai parcouru l'ouvrage que vous m'avez envoyé hier et, vraiment, j'ai été content de l'édition; ce n'est pas encore le moment de donner mon avis sur la valeur de l'œuvre en elle-même. Ici vous n'auriez trouvé, en fait d'ouvrages du R. P. Louis-Marie d'Ameno, que son livre: Practica criminalis Minorum; *le* De Delictis et Pœnis *se trouve, je crois, dans un autre de nos couvents; mais vous auriez reçu un excellent accueil. Je crois que Des Grieux n'a guère habité le Saint-Sulpice actuel, qui ne date que de 1816.*

J'ai remarqué, à la page 132–133, une erreur de traduction assez grave: vous rendez Carthusia Ticinensis *par Chartreuse du Tessin, quand il s'agit de la fameuse Chartreuse de Pavie, fort connue de tous les voyageurs en Italie. Il y a aussi, autant qu'un coup d'œil superficiel m'a permis de m'en rendre compte, quelques autres erreurs; mais, en somme, l'œuvre est bonne, et vous pouvez recevoir les félicitations de*
Votre tout petit serviteur,

Fr. A.....
o. m. c.
m. p.
Couvent des Capucins, rue...

About Sinistrari

VAMzzz Publishing

Incubi &
succubi, a
special class
of astral
wildlife...

Ludovico Maria Sinistrari de Ameno and his DÆMONIALITAS

Ludovico Maria Sinistrari, author of *De Dæmonialitate, et Incubis, et Succubis,* was born on February 26, 1622 in Ameno, Italy. He studied in Pavia and entered the Franciscan Order in 1647. He taught philosophy and theology to students in Pavia, some of them having been attracted to the area by his fame.

Sinistrari was an advisor to the Supreme Sacred Congregation of the Roman and Universal Inquisition in Rome. He was considered an expert on exorcism and wrote about the effects (during exorcisms) of various plants and other substances including cubeb, cardamom, ginger and nutmeg. He was also considered an expert on demonology, sins relating to sexuality, and especially all combinations thereof (demonilatria), including investigations of those individuals accused of sexual relations with demons. Allegations along these lines influenced later Inquisition investigations of those accused of witchcraft. His advice was, at various times, directed against enemies of the Roman Catholic Church, including Martin Luther, whom he referred to as a "devil-begotten man".

Sinistrari was a prolific author and was responsible for many of the works which framed Inquisition thinking during the 17th century, particularly regarding the incubus, succubus and other demons which were thought to roam the Earth, with their sinful sexual practices. He also published about "sexual sins" in general, but with the accent on homosexuality *(Lewdness)* and sodomy in *Peccatum Mutum (The Mute Sin)* – which saw its first publication long after his death 1893.

In 1700, a year before his death, Sinistrari published *De Delictis et Poenis Tractatus Absolutissimus (The Most Absolute Treatise of Crime and Punishment)* - which he had started in 1688. Despite being asked to complete the work for the Franciscan order as a general criminal code-book and despite Sinistrari's work for the Inquisition, the book was added to the Index Librorum Prohibitorum in 1709 and banned. Most likely because it dealt with issues relating to the qualification of judges. Five pages of this last mentioned work are, by the way, also dedicated to the demonolatria-problem.

Alexandra H. M. Nagel [1] showed that the translation of Sinistrari's *De Dæmonialitate, et Incubis, et Succubis* by Liseux, has been known to some famous writers with an interest in the occult. Madame Blavatsky referred to the work, Joris-Karl Huysmans consulted it for his novel *Là-bas*. Ezra Pound

'Sinistrari was an advisor to the Supreme Sacred Congregation of the Roman and Universal Inquisition in Rome.'

linked it in 1909 to the fairies and spirits in William B. Yeats' *The Celtic Twilight*, while Yeats himself made use of it in his notes to *Visions and Beliefs* in the West of Ireland by Lady Augusta Gregory. Rev. Montague Summers, critical about Liseux' translation, created his own English version of the work.

Both Sinistrari's original and the translation of Lisieux, have been subject to academic discussions and controversy. This resulted in the conclusion that Sinistrari's *De Dæmonialitate, et Incubis, et Succubis* is indeed authentic, but the author probably composed the book, by lending material from another writer and adding it to his own.

In 1986 Carlo Carena published an Italian translation *(Demonialità: Ossia possibilità, modo e varietà dell'unione carnaledell'uomo col demonio).*

Note:
1. Tracing the mysterious facts in Isidore Liseux' publication of *De Daemonialitate* by Ludovico M. Sinistrari, December 23, 2008

Isodore Liseux

The manuscript of *De Dæmonialitate, et Incubis, et Succubis* was discovered by the French bibliophile and publisher of erotica and curiosa, Isidore Liseux (1835 - 1894). Liseux was active as publisher in Paris in the last quarter of the 19th century. His publications, which were usually translated and annotated by his friend Alcide Bonneau or by Liseux himself, were mostly rare texts of 16th till 18th century authors: hard to find and little known books, republished in juxtalinear translation (Latin-French or Italian-French).

Liseux and Bonneau were both ex-priests and knew each other since seminary. His books were published in small numbers, on high quality paper, and with excellent typography printed by Claude Motteroz, Antoine Bécus, and later Charles Unsinger.

'Sinistrari also published about "sexual sins" in general, but with the accent on homosexuality and sodomy.'

Incubi and Succubi; not dead yet!
(by Benjamin Adamah)

"For proofe hereof James Sprenger and Institor affirme, that manie times witches are seene in the fields, and woods, prostituting themselves uncovered and naked up to the navill, wagging and mooving their members in everie part, according to the disposition of one being about that act of concupiscence, and yet nothing seene of the beholders upon hir; saving that after such a convenient time as is required about such a peece of worke, a blacke vapor of the length and bignesse of a man, hath beene seene as it were to depart from hir, and to ascend from that place."
– Reginald Scot in his *Discoverie of Witchcraft* (1584) quoting from the *Malleus Maleficarum*.

Incubus

One of the more interesting things about *Demoniality* is the suggestion that incubi and/or succubi are not by definition the evil spirits as portrayed in modern horror movies. When I read the book much of their features and behaviour brought into my memory several poltergeist anecdotes as described by Harry Price in *Poltergeist – Tales of the Supernatural.* They also reminded me of some land, fertility and forest spirits described in the volumes of Wilhelm Mannhardt *(die Korndämonen; Wald und Feldkulte; etc.),* and recently in several books of Claude Lecouteux. The link with certain Elementals (nature spirits) is very strong. This probably accounts for the fact that exorcisms, holy objects and Jesus Christ, don't seem to make much impression on the creature, according to reports of those dedicated priests who tried to expel it.

'Robert Bruce classifies the incubus/succubus under astral wildlife.'

The most interesting and plausible description I ever read of the incubus, comes from the Australian metaphysic and out of body-expert Robert Bruce. He classifies the incubus/succubus under astral wildlife and regards the creature as a special class, not a priori evil or parasitical, that simply lives of human (and perhaps animal) sexual energy by directly stimulating the sex chakra area. One can argue about the fact whether the often simultaneously occurring extremely erotic dreams during an incubus or succubus attack, are the result of this energetic stimulation or are caused by telepathically projected images. His astral sight picture of the creature is that of a transparent entity, oval shaped, like an elongated rugby ball, that can change colour, mostly towards red or reddish, with a flower shaped end, by which it moves through the astral realm, which looks a bit like the lower of a daisy. The size Bruce gives varies between 18 inches – 3 feet or about 40 – 90 cm.

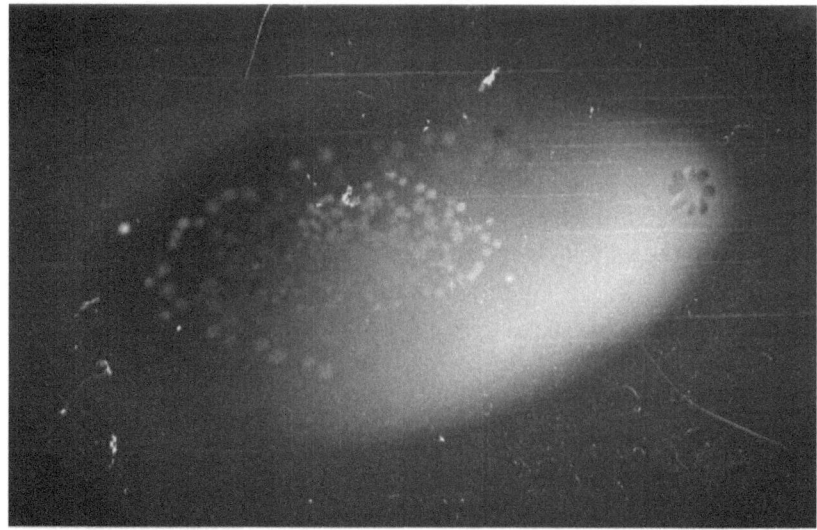

Astral shape incubus

The odd thing about the incubus/succubus experience is that both men and women can have them, and many people still have them today. So we should not treat this as an outdated phenomenon locked in medieval times or the Renaissance, or ancient Mesopotamia, where they already were recognized as a special class of sex spirits, called the Lilim.

Jewish culture created an extended version of the Lilim-spirit, via their demonisation of the ancient goddess Lilith in synergy with the taboo on masturbation and young Jewish men in the peak days of their testosterone level. Lilith became a succuba, or female sex demon, and the main cause of wet dreams and concentration problems. Even worse, she became associated with predator-demon focused on harming or killing babies. As a tulpa-derivate of the original (lotus)goddess, this seems to work out as a self fulfilling cultural prophesy.

After the horrible connotation and contexts the creature received as a stigma, during the witch prosecutions, there was a period of silence and a fading away from the collective consciousness. Then incubus/succubus grew in popularity at the end of the 18th century. This was due to a Swiss painter, living in political exile in England and with certain frustrations in his love life. Heinrich Füssli aka Henry Fuseli painted his first version of *The Nightmare* or *Incubus* in 1781, showing a sleeping woman with an apelike demon on her chest and a ghostly mare sticking her head through the curtains of her bedroom. In the period 1780-1790 Fuseli was very interested in the occult. He was also in love with Anna Landolt, the niece of his friend Lavater, but she rejected him, probably because she was already engaged to someone else. Anna Landolt could have been very well

'We should not treat this as an outdated phenomenon locked in medieval times, since many people still have the incubus/succubus experience today.'

the real secret behind the power of the Fuseli's *Incubus* and the amazing popularity the work has kept ever since. The 1781 version of the work has her portrait depicted on the backside of the canvas – invisible to the visitors of the Detroit Institute of Arts.

It is unclear why artists started to portray the incubus-nightmare combination as an apelike creature. However, many people who frequently experience out of body sessions, reported seeing gargoyle-like creatures who acted as some sort of dimension-watchers. They were more or less apelike, but they were not incubi or succubi.

Fuseli fused the sexual aspect of the incubus with the nightmare and sleeping paralyses experience. Explaining the sleeping paralysis in sec medical or neurological terms is of course possible, but it would be dishonest to state this perspective as the only correct one. Therefore, there are too many experiences of actually feeling an entity sitting on one's chest. I have had once such an experience myself, whereby I could actually grab the creature's arm and hold it for several seconds before it dematerialised. People, especially women, can have an experience of actually feeling sexually stimulated, or being pushed out of their physical body. Historical reports are, despite the fantasies of the Inquisition and their outstanding skills to politicize them, full of "very material" manifesting incubi and succubi. Even Pico della Mirandolo spent some ink on the subject. He reported on a man who had a relation with a succubus for over 40 years, who said he would rather die than stop this relation. Delassus in his *Les Incubus*

Incubus

(1897) writes about a twenty year old girl who couldn't concentrate on God because of an incubus who brought her in the most delirious sexual state of arousal. The exorcism performed on her failed, because she didn't really want to get rid of the incubus. The most remarkable anecdote concerns a brothel in Bologna, where a number of succubi were actually "exploited". The orgasms triggered by these creatures are usually described as "breathtaking heavenly intense". Even more remarkable however, is that the operator of the brothel was actually sentenced to death in 1468 for this "crime".

By the way, you could easily protect yourself against incubi and succubi, by wearing a red peony, a peony root, a piece of red coral or by carrying a red jasper or pebble in your pocket...

Paper books

VAMzzz Publishing

VAMzzz Publishing is located in the very centre of old Amsterdam, in The Netherlands. Our publishing company creates high quality revised editions of five star occult, witchcraft, Gothic and esoteric classics, mostly written in the Fin de siècle-period and early 20th century.

As a publisher, we deeply respect the writer of any book we choose, so we join our forces (top level graphic design & thirty years of occult studies) to produce enchanting volumes which maximize the reading pleasure and inform, often with extra added information. In contrast to the current trend of digital screen addiction, we think, this variety of literature needs to be presented on paper. *No e-books, but real books!*

Apart from re-publications of valuable but forgotten books, we are also in the preparation of new publications on topics such as self-healing, magic, new astrology and more.

VAMzzz Publishing
P.O. Box 3340
1001 AC Amsterdam
The Netherlands
contactvamzzz@gmail.com
www.vamzzz.com

Previews of all books including a complete table of contents can be viewed on www.vamzzz.com. More books will be added to the list. Please visit our website regularly for the latest updates.

Recommended

PAN Magazine
by VAMzzz Publishing
Free Online
www.vamzzz.com/pan.html

In Greek religion and mythology, PAN, the companion of the nymphs, is the god of the wild, shepherds and flocks, wild mountains and rustic music. He has the hindquarters, legs and horns of a goat, in the same manner as a faun or satyr. He is also recognized as the god of fields, groves and wooded glens; connected to fertility, the joy of life itself and the season of spring.

Though a mortal god in antiquity and an underground witch-god in medieval times, the last decades PAN has become a patron of both modern occultism, Wicca, paganism and the green guerilla – enthroned again as the one and only God of the Earth and Nature. PAN is the vibe touching those who refuse to become part of a machine, and who remain loyal to Mother Nature, the visible and hidden one. Therefore PAN is the most suitable icon we could chose for this periodical.

The Banshee
A Ghost Hunter's Investigation
by Elliot O'Donnell
222 pages, Paperback, ISBN 9789492355232

The banshee is a mysterious female spirit in Irish folklore, who heralds the death of a family member, usually by shrieking or keening. The screeching sound is described as somewhere between the wail of a woman and the moan of an owl, a low singing or piercing loud and able to break glass. The banshee appears as an old hag or beautiful lady, but may also appear as a crow, stoat, hare and weasel - animals associated in Ireland with witchcraft.

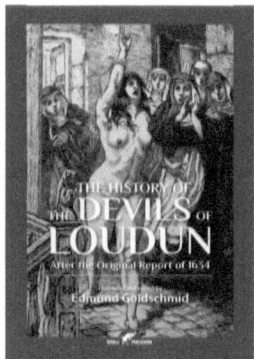

The History of the Devils of Loudun
After the Original Report of 1634
Translation by Edmund Goldschmid
118 pages, Paperback, ISBN 9789492355256

Around 1632 seventeen Ursuline Nuns were taken over by demons and went into a sexual and blasphemous state of hysteria for years. The work also describes the trial of a womanizing local priest named Father Urbain Grandier, who was accused of summoning these demons and, in the end, burned at the stake.

Religion and Lust
or The Physical Correlation of Religious Emotion and Sexual Desire
by James Weir Jr.
146 pages, Paperback, ISBN 9789492355270

In *Religion and Lust,* author James Weir Jr. investigates the origins of religious feeling, the once world wide spread fertility worship and the physical correlation of religious emotion and sexual desire. A major part of the work is filled with a colourful collection of religious or semi-religious, sexual rites, once practiced all over the globe, connecting the most "primitive" tribe to the most "civilized" nations.

Incubi and Succubi or Demoniality
A Historical Study of Sexual Contacts with Demons
by Sinistrari of Ameno
194 pages, Paperback, ISBN 9789492355263

This book is a revised English edition of Sinistrari's fascinating 17th century study on the orgasm-stimulating sex demon. The incubus and succubus are the same creature. The incubus is its male shape, copulates with women. The succubus visits men, triggering wet dreams. The intercourse with this astral visitor was called demoniality, a term no longer in use, though nowadays people are still having these mysterious incubus/succubus-"sexperiences".

Mysteria
History of the Secret Doctrines & Mystic Rites of Ancient Religions & Medieval and Modern Secret Orders
by Dr. Otto Henne am Rhyn
288 pages, Paperback, ISBN 9789492355225

Mysteria is a treasure box of missing conspiracy links and one of the very few publications, which offer reliable information about Adam Weishaupt's Illuminati for "the web & media-disinformed". Lodge-insider Otto Henne am Rhyn takes you on a journey, back to the Mystery cults of ancient Egypt, Babylon and Greece, passes Templars and explains modern lodges.

Magic and Magical Fetish
by Alfred Cort Haddon
108 pages, Paperback, ISBN 9789492355300

Alfred C. Haddon gives a practical and theoretical insight of the universal principles of magic, categorized in different techniques. The book is one of the very few works ever published, which describes wind and rain making. Magic is divided into sympathetic magic, the magic of words, talismans and divination, magical training routines. A kaleidoscope of forgotten magical techniques, which wasn't available for decades.

The Eleusian and Bacchic Mysteries
A Dissertation
by Thomas Taylor
200 pages, Paperback, ISBN 9789492355294

The Eleusian and Bacchic Mysteries focus on life, death and rebirth in a living nature (the present), while this nature was regarded as the converging of past and future. Taylor describes a series of lost secret rites. These rites were once the appointed means for regeneration through an inner union with the Divine Essence, despite their wild and sexual aspect.

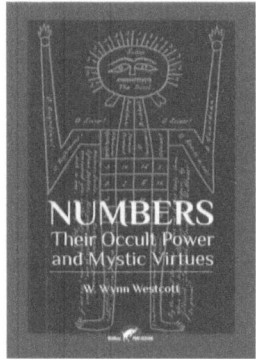

Numbers
Their Occult Power and Mystic Virtues
by W. Wynn Westcott
170 pages, Paperback, ISBN 9789492355287

This book may be regarded as the "bible of numerology". It deals with Pythagorean number divisions, explains 3 different kinds of Kabalistic numerology, and reveals the hidden logic and symbolism of the numbers 1,2,3,4,5,6,7,8,9,10,11,12 and 13. This is accompanied by a long course of numbers between 14 and 25920. Special symbolisms are included like the link between numbers and planets and numbers in relation to the Apocalypse.

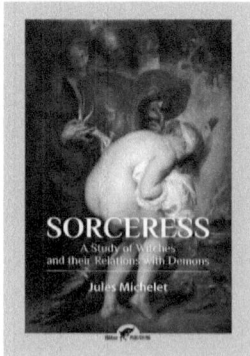

Sorceress
A Study of Witches and their Relations with Demons
by Jules Michelet
432 pages, Paperback, ISBN 9789492355249

This work is one of the most vivid, dark and confronting studies on witchcraft ever produced. Long before Murray's Witch-Cult in Western Europe, Michelet positions the medieval witch within a diminishing ancient culture of nature worship and the ruthless efforts of Christianity, with its cruel hostility towards nature, life (and women), to overwrite it. A nightmare of the most extraordinary verisimilitude and poetical power...

Aradia
Gospel of the Witches
by Charles Godfrey Leland
174 pages, Paperback, ISBN 9789492355010

This wonderful book describes the creation according to Italian witch-lore. We also read about the witch-meeting or sabbath (treguenda) and the book contains many original magical recipes, like spells for love and good fortune. Diana is further connected to the Moon and the fairy world.

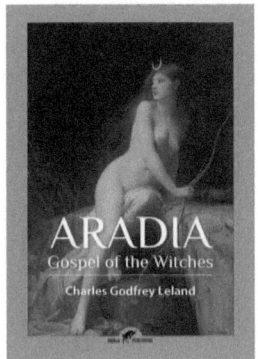

Demonology and Devil-Lore *(Volume 1)*
by Moncure Daniel Conway
490 pages, Paperback, ISBN 9789492355157

Demonology and Devil-Lore *(Volume 2)*
by Moncure Daniel Conway
518 pages, Paperback, ISBN 9789492355164

Within the demonology scope, this rare and mostly forgotten, almost 1000 pages thick masterpiece, remains unsurpassed in quality and completeness. Even in the 21st century the works offer fascinating missing links for both the academic and student of occult traditions. Moncure Daniel Conway divides Volume 1 in three parts and deals mainly with the evolution and thematic classification of ex-gods, demons and nature creatures. Volume 2 deals primarily with the diabolic and with the Devil himself, his ethnic history and connected topics.

Fairy Mythology *(Volume 1)*
Romance and Superstition of Various Countries 1
by Thomas Keightley
404 pages, Paperback, ISBN 9789492355096

Fairy Mythology *(Volume 2)*
Romance and Superstition of Various Countries 2
by Thomas Keightley
404 pages, Paperback, ISBN 9789492355102

The term Fairy covers all kinds of nature spirits, not just the tiny sugarsweet creatures hovering around flowers. A unique and impressive book on this subject, published in a revised 2 volume-edition. No wiccan or pagan can afford to leave these books unopened. About Elves, Dwarfs, Kobolds, Trolls, Changelings, Meremaids, Nisses, Fairies, Brownies, Puck and other Elemental spirits all over the world.

Etruscan Magic & Occult Remedies
(Two volumes in one book)
by Charles Godfrey Leland
628 pages, Paperback, ISBN 9789492355003

Part One of the book gives us a complete and detailed insight in the Etruscan and Roman rooted pantheon of the Tuscan Streghe (witches). Part Two describes many of their spells, incantations, sorcery and several lost divination methods. Much information in this book, Leland received first hand from the Tuscan witches Maddalena and Marietta.

Voodoos and Obeahs
Phases of West India Witchcraft
by Joseph J. Williams
374 pages, Paperback, ISBN 9789492355119

This work goes into great depth concerning the New World-African connection and is highly recommended if you want a deep understanding of the dramatic historical background of Haitian and Jamaican magic and witchcraft, and the profound influence of imperialism, slavery and racism on its development. Williams includes numerous quotations from rare documents and books on the topic.

Devil-worship in France
Or The Question of Lucifer
by Arthur Edward Waite
240 pages, Paperback, ISBN 9789492355065

In *Devil-Worship in France,* Waite attempts to discern what is genuine from what is fake in the evidence of 19th century Satanism. To get the answers he spends a great deal of time investigating the French Masonic echelon, debunking a "conspiracy of falsehood" and determining what should be understood by Satanism and what not. Huysmans' diabolical novel *Là-Bas* (1891) inspired Waite to write this sceptical analysis.

Testament of Solomon
A First Century AD Grimoire
76 pages, Paperback, ISBN 9789492355041

A first century AD grimoire, and therefore the oldest, and least known, of all grimoires (magical instruction books) in the occult tradition. The book describes health inflicting demons of zodiacal decans, summoned by King Solomon, and how he controlled them to use their forces to build his temple and more. Translated by F. C. Conybeare, appeared first in the *Jewish Quarterly Review* of October, 1898.

Ophiolatreia
Rites and Mysteries of Serpent Worship
by Hargrave Jennings
186 pages, Paperback, ISBN 9789492355126

An account of the rites and mysteries connected with the origin, rise and development of serpent worship in various parts of the world, enriched with interesting traditions, and a full description of the celebrated serpent mounds & temples, the whole forming an exposition of one of the phases of phallic, or sex worship.

Anansi
Jamaican stories of the Spider God
by Martha Warren Beckwith
494 pages, Paperback, ISBN 9789492355171

Anansi is both a god, spirit and African folktale character. He often takes the shape of a spider and is considered to be the spirit of all knowledge of stories. He is also one of the most important characters of West African and Caribbean folklore.

Spiritual Fetichism
A Study of West African Culture, Witchcraft, Magic & Demonology
by Robert Hamill Nassau
524 pages, Paperback, ISBN 9789492355188

Despite a nowadays anachronist and disturbing perspective, the book has remained most valuable for students of the occult, especially those interested in demonology, voodoo, hoodoo and its roots, African magick and religion, witchcraft, the classes of African spirits, and of course the spiritual and magickal use of a fetish.

Là-Bas
A Journey into the Self
by Joris-Karl Huysmans
378 pages, Paperback, ISBN 9789492355058

The plot of *Là-Bas* concerns the novelist Durtal, who is disgusted by the emptiness and vulgarity of the modern world. He seeks relief by turning to the study of the Middle Ages. Through his contacts in Paris, Durtal discovers that Satanism is not a thing of the past but alive and kicking in turn of the century France. The novel culminates with a description of a black mass.

Unicorn
A mythological investigation
by Robert Brown Jr.
124 pages, Paperback, ISBN 9789492355072

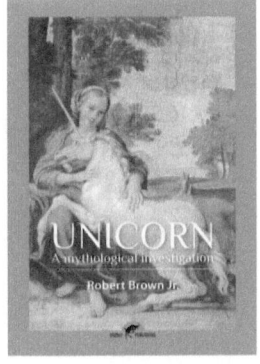

Brown Jr. believes the unicorn to be a lunar symbol, and draws on mythology from a wide range of sources all over the world to build his case. The author discusses the heraldic use of the unicorn, relates the creature to ancient goddesses like Astarte, Hecate en the Gorgon Medusa, and provides the reader with lost esoteric Moon-lore.

The House of Souls
A Fragment of Life / The White People
The Great God Pan / The Inmost Light
by Arthur Machen
336 pages, Paperback, ISBN 9789492355218

A collection of four masterpieces of horror and mystery, first collectively published in 1906. In the ingenious plot of *The Great God Pan,* a young woman is forced into Pan's reality, and turns into a femme fatale. *The Inmost Light* involves a doctor's scientific experiments into occultism and a vampiric force. In *The White People* a young girl's diary is discovered, describing her initiation into a secret world of folklore and ritual magic. In *A Fragment of Life* Machen tries to convince us of a hidden reality.

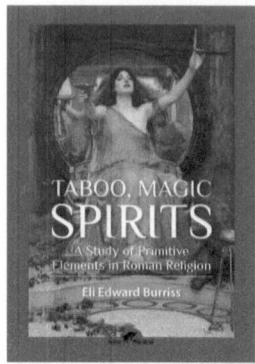

Taboo, Magic, Spirits
A study of primitive elements in Roman religion
by Eli Edward Burriss
200 pages, Paperback, ISBN 9789492355034

In Ancient Rome Mana was the term used for a mysterious, magical medium, which could be helpful or harmful (Taboo). Just like the Chinese qi, it could empower the positive and the negative. Contents: Mana, Magic and Animism – Positive and Negative Mana (Taboo) – Miscellaneous Taboos – Magic Acts: The General Principles – Removing Evils by - Magic Acts – Incantation and Prayer– Naturalism and Animism.

Chaldean Magic
It's Origin and Development
by François Lenormant
454 pages, Paperback, ISBN 9789492355027

The essentials of magic in Chaldea are presented inside a context of comparison or contrast to Egyptian, Median, Turanian, Finno-Tartarian and Akkadian magic, mythologies, religion and speech. Interesting is the Chaldean demonology, with its incubus, succubus, vampire, nightmare and many Elemental spirits, most of them coalesced with the primal powers of nature.

Amazons - *Two publications in one book* -
I. The Amazons by Guy Cadogan Rothery
II. Religious Cults Associated With the Amazons
    by Florence Mary Bennett
328 pages, Paperback, ISBN 9789492355089

Contents I: The Amazons of Antiquity – Amazons in Far Asia – Modern Amazons of the Caucasus – Amazons of Europe – Amazons of Africa – Amazons of America – The Amazon Stones. Contents II: The Amazons in Greek legend – The Great Mother – Ephesian Artemis – Artemis Astrateia and Apollo Amazonius – Ares.

www.ingramcontent.com/pod-product-compliance
Lightning Source LLC
Chambersburg PA
CBHW020246130626
46549CB00005B/2080